spiritualized

a look inside the teenage soul

BY MARK HEALY

D1737032

AlloyBooks

Dedication: This book is dedicated to the humbling, hopeful notion that compassion rules and that love is everywhere if you know where to let it find you.

Acknowledgments: I owe an immeasurable debt of gratitude to the smart, kind, unique souls who took the time and had the courage to tell me their stories. Thank you! Finding the right storytellers was half the effort, and the following people were extremely helpful: Craig Gordon, Zuhara Calhoun, Ayanna Byrd, Eleni Gage, Jim Ehrenhaft, Michael Doran, Tarika Huhadeen, Jonathan Linton, Rabbi Mindy Portnoy, and Naika Renee. Thanks again. Thanks also to Professor Robert Thurman, Bishop Chilton Knudsen, and Rabbi Jefferey Salkin for sharing your knowledge and wisdom. Thanks to Susan Kaplow, Matt Diamond, Jim Johnson, Sam Gradess, Jodi Smith, and the rest of the Alloy community for the vision and the opportunity.

Special gratitude goes to Lauren Monchik for making the book look miraculously good, Tucker Shaw for making it fun, and Ann Brashares and everyone at 17th Street for making it work—especially Jodi Anderson, who improved this book enormously while exhibiting the patience and dedication of a truly evolved soul. Thank you.

248.B HEA 32020727

ALLOY BOOKS
Published by the Penguin Group
Penguin Putnam Books for Young Readers,
345 Hudson Street, New York, New York 10014, U.S.A.

Published by Puffin Books,
a division of Penguin Putnam Books for Young Readers, 2000

10 9 8 7 6 5 4 3 2 1

Copyright © 17th Street Productions, an Alloy Online, Inc. company, 2000
All rights reserved

Cover design by Russell Gordon
Interior design by Jan Derevjanik

Produced by 17th Street Productions,
an Alloy Online, Inc. company
33 West 17th Street
New York, NY 10011

Alloy, Alloy.com, AlloyBooks, and 17th Street Productions and associated logos
are trademarks and/or registered trademarks of Alloy Online, Inc.

ISBN 0-14-131018-9
Printed in the United States of America

contents

introduction

You hear about spirituality all the time: spiritual experiences, spiritual journeys, finding the spirit within. But what does "spirituality" really mean? Well, it depends on who you ask. There are at least as many ways to define, explore, understand, and express spirituality as there are individual people on the planet.

In *Spiritualized* you'll get an intimate look inside the intensely personal spiritual lives of fifteen teens from all over the map. Some of them have decided to stick with the beliefs they were raised with. Some have embraced the beliefs of other faiths. Others have broken away and created their own set of values. And still others are beginning to discover, for the first time, that spirituality has a meaningful place in their lives at all.

Spiritualized is a series of snapshots, a glimpse into the way spirituality fits into the lives of each of these teens—whether that's through an established religion or a custom-made set of beliefs. But while you'll find these pages loaded with background info on the religions discussed, this book is not a comprehensive explanation of any one faith or religious creed. And it's not a complete overview of the world's religions—there are far too many to include. It's not so much a look at the beliefs as a look at the believers.

What these teens say and do may surprise you; learning their beliefs may enlighten you; hearing their stories may inspire you. It all depends.

What do *you* believe?

aminah

Aminah Abdul-Musawwir

Hometown: Boston, Massachusetts

Age: 17

Gender: Female

School/Grade: High School Senior (Home Schooled)

Raised: Muslim

Currently: Muslim

Aminah Abdul-Musawwir likes to dance and hang out with her friends. She loves scary movies, scarier books—like Stephen King's—and kickboxing. In a lot of ways she's a typical seventeen-year-old, and in a lot of ways she isn't. For starters, she's home schooled by her mom and a tutor who comes to her house. She doesn't date, curse, or wear clothes that are, by her religion's standards, too short or too tight. Aminah is a Muslim who is studying the Qur'an, the sacred text of Islam. Her parents both converted to Islam before she was born. Aminah is learning to read and write Arabic so she can understand the Qur'an better. But as difficult as learning Arabic is, it's not as hard as explaining to her peers what being a Muslim is all about.

religion: islam

Founder: None. Muslims believe that Islam was established on the first day of creation.

History: According to Islamic texts, in the seventh century A.D. the prophet Muhammad received messages from God to preach to the people. The messages introduced his followers to Allah, furthering the teachings of the prophets who came before him, among them Moses and Jesus Christ.

Beliefs: In Arabic the word Islam means "to surrender," indicating followers' willingness to surrender to the will of their god, Allah. Islam is founded on the guiding rituals called the Five Pillars, which demand that all Muslims believe in the statement "There is no god but God, and Muhammad is his prophet"; practice regular prayer, conducted five times a day while facing the holy city of Mecca; give alms to the poor; keep the fast of Ramadan; and make a pilgrimage at least once in a lifetime to Mecca, if possible.

Muslims believe in the promise of eternal life. They follow the teachings of the Qur'an, coupled with a behavior code called Islamic law, which forbids Muslims from eating pork and meat from animals that were not killed in the proper way. Muslims also put a high premium on chastity (particularly for women) and do not believe in extramarital sex. Members of the opposite sex do not spend time alone together after puberty. Women must dress modestly in clothing that is not tight or see-through and must cover their hair with scarves.

Big Books: The Qur'an (or Koran) is the holiest text.

House of Worship: Mosque.

Holidays: The holiest Muslim holiday is Ramadan, a month-long period of atonement during which Muslims fast from dawn to dusk and are not allowed to smoke, drink alcohol (which is, in fact, forbidden throughout the year), or have sex. This holiday is followed by 'Id Al-Fitr, a feast that marks the end of Ramadan and the beginning of the Muslim new year.

Sects: The two major Muslim sects are the Sunni and the Shiite.

We must build dikes of courage

A LOT OF RELIGIONS HAVE RESTRICTIONS AND RULES REGARDING DIET, DRESS, AND CONDUCT. WHAT KIND OF RULES DO YOU HAVE TO FOLLOW AS A MUSLIM?

We don't eat pork because the Qur'an says we're not supposed to—it's forbidden to us. (I don't like the way it smells, anyway.) We're not allowed to drink, smoke, or put any impurities into our bodies. And no tattoos, either. There are a lot of things that we're not allowed to do, like go to clubs because of the mixture of boys and girls.

IS IT HARD TO ADHERE TO ALL OF THOSE RULES AT THIS POINT IN YOUR LIFE?

Being a teenager, it is really hard. At this age I think, That really sucks, or ask, "Why can't I do this or do that?" but when I really think about it, the rules make sense to me. Still, sometimes you tell yourself, "Okay, I can do this now because I'm in my teens, but when I'm older, I'm gonna do the right thing," but you never know if that's going to happen. You just have to try to get your priorities straight here and now. It's challenging day by day, but I feel like I've made a lot of the right decisions, and I'm really looking forward to being the best I can be as a Muslim.

ARE THERE ANY RULES YOU'VE FOUND PARTICULARLY DIFFICULT TO DEAL WITH?

I'm not allowed to wear short or tight clothes, and that kind of pissed me off for a while because my friends and I would go to the beach and I'd be the one in khakis and a T-shirt. But when I really think about it, bikinis are unappealing to me. I know how my guy friends look at the girls wearing bikinis, and I don't want to be looked at like that, so maybe it's good that I don't get to dress like that.

WHAT ABOUT DATING?

If you're truly interested in someone, you can go to your parents and let them know how you're feeling, and you might be able to get engaged at a young age. That way the relationship will be *halal,* which means "allowed," as opposed to *haram,* which means "forbidden." It's forbidden for Muslims to have sex outside of marriage. For me it's kind of scary to think, How am I going to marry someone I haven't gone out with? But I think that when you approach the situation in the right way, all right will come out of it. In this case, marriage is the right way.

HAVE YOU HAD BOYFRIENDS BEFORE?

I have had male friends before, and that's bending the rules. I really shouldn't have. We all make mistakes. I learned that there are reasons why we as Muslims, and anyone for that matter, should and should not do things that are unlawful for us—that there are good reasons why certain things are allowed and others are not. Being young and sometimes unaware, we tend to bend the rules and hope to benefit from it, when in fact it's nothing more than a mistake—and for some, a lesson to be learned the hard way.

What if God was one of us?—Joan Osborne

pilgrimages

The faithful make pilgrimages for many reasons—to show devotion, to ask for divine guidance, to see important religious sites, to do penance, or to reenact journeys that are important to their faith. Usually pilgrims go to the holiest spots—the birthplace of their religion, the home of a saint or mystic, or the site of some important miracle. In some religions, pilgrimages are mandatory. One of the Pillars of Islam requires a *hajj*, a pilgrimage to the holy land of Mecca in Saudi Arabia. Every adult Muslim must go once in his or her life if he or she is well enough and can afford the trip. Once there, Muslims perform a number of rituals, including shaving their heads. Jerusalem is an extremely important destination for Jews, Christians, and Muslims. Millions of travelers head there every year—Christians go because the location is significant to the life of their messiah, Jesus Christ; Jews travel there to visit the Western Wall; Muslims go for the important mosques. They all go to show their devotion and to ask for guidance. Pilgrimages also offer followers a way to get in touch with the roots of their religion. Every summer teenage Mormons trace the roots of their founder, Joseph Smith, from Utah to Ohio and to upstate New York. Buddhists frequently travel to the places that mark the milestones of the life of their founder, Buddha Gotama—his birthplace, the site of his first sermon, and the spot where he attained enlightenment.

aminah on modesty:

The need for modesty in Muslims is the same in both men and women. But on account of the differences between the sexes, a greater amount of privacy is required for women than for men, especially in matters of dress. For example, on the beach (or anywhere except the mosque and in prayer), it would be permissible for men to wear shorts that reach the knees. This dress would also be permissible for women, but only when they are around other women, and of course, women should cover up their chests as well. Modesty is considered good form for Muslims. Its purpose is not only to guard women, but also to guard the spiritual good of men. It's all about honoring yourself and showing the proper self-respect.

SO IN ORDER TO BE A GOOD MUSLIM, YOU SOMETIMES HAVE TO ACCEPT RULES YOU MAY NOT UNDERSTAND. THAT REQUIRES A LOT OF FAITH.

My faith is tested every day. It's so much easier to do something that's wrong than to do something that's right. And my parents don't force the rules on me—so it's up to me to make the right decisions. I think what saves me—and it might seem corny—is to just meditate. To just sit and pray and

Humility has that low sweet root,

actually think about doing something before I do it. I know myself. For example, I love dancing, and I know that if I went to a club, I'd probably dance with lots of guys. I know what it's going to lead up to. So I've got to think about it first and hold back ahead of time.

DOES ADHERING TO ALL OF THESE RULES EVER MAKE IT HARD TO HAVE FUN?

It's not like I'm not going to have fun. I try to give myself alternatives. I'll say, "I'm not going to that club tonight, so I'll go to the movies with my friends instead," or, "Okay, I love to dance, so I'll take dance lessons." Or, "I love to swim, but I can't go to the beach with all my friends and wear a bathing suit, so I'll take swimming classes with some of my other friends at the YWCA where there are only women." I love lots of things—scary movies, scary books, and kickboxing. I love writing short stories and poetry. I'm gonna have fun; I'm just gonna have fun in a different way. Everything you do portrays who you are. So as a Muslim, everything you do has to be in an Islamic way.

MUSLIMS ARE SUPPOSED TO FAST DURING THE MONTH OF RAMADAN. DOES DOING THIS MAKE YOU MORE SPIRITU-ALLY CONNECTED?

Yes, it really does. Ramadan is a month to remember your lord, so you read the Qur'an more. You're fasting every day from sunup to sundown—so you're not jumping around being crazy. It's a whole spiritual thing because when you take your time away from eating, it's almost like you're a whole different person. Obesity is such a big problem here in the United States because people eat so much. We waste so much time and money on food. It's good to get away from that.

HOW DO YOU FEEL DURING RAMADAN?

I feel smarter when I wake up before the sunrise to eat and pray. The whole process of Ramadan is good for the mind, body, and soul. I love getting up really early in the morning. It's such a peaceful time, when the whole family goes down to eat before the sun comes up. I love it when we get together and eat and then we pray. Then when the sun goes down at night, we eat together and we pray again. We're all so busy—people are working, my brothers have baseball practice, or this or that—we hardly ever pray together, so it's really nice when we do.

MUSLIMS ARE REQUIRED TO PRAY AT FIVE SPECIFIC TIMES EACH DAY. DO YOU ALWAYS PRAY WHEN YOU'RE SUPPOSED TO?

I'd be lying if I told you that I always pray exactly when I should, but if I miss one of the five daily prayers, I always make it up. When I do my prayers five times a day, I'm more calm, collected, and content. Praying reminds me of why I'm here on this earth.

WHY DO YOU THINK YOU'RE HERE?

It's a test—there is a heaven and hell. There's this saying that I really love, and I always repeat it: "Don't give up the next world for this world. Give up this world for the next world." This life is not gonna be forever. Use your faith and take time out to pray and do things that are gonna add up. And make a difference in the hereafter. That's what keeps me on point. Sometimes your faith can get a little frayed. You start thinking, What if this isn't the right religion? or, What if I'm supposed to be doing something else? But I think as long as you know that you're doing something that's right, you're okay. Praying can't be wrong; helping somebody out can't be wrong; making somebody happy can't be wrong. So you just try and do your best.

WHAT DO YOU THINK IS THE MOST COMMON MISUNDER-STANDING ABOUT ISLAM?

I think a lot of people confuse Islam with Middle Eastern culture. They're two separate things. I'm a Muslim, but I'm also American, you know? I'm

African-American, German, Dutch, and Native American.

WHY DO YOU THINK THERE ARE SO MANY MISUNDER-STANDINGS ABOUT YOUR RELIGION?

Some people are just kind of ignorant about it. I've had people come up to me and ask me if I cover my head because my hair is ugly. These people don't know much about Islam, and if you try to tell them about it, they think that you're just being pushy. When I talk about my religion, I just want to let people know what we're about, you know? I try to explain to my Christian and Jewish friends that our religions are so much alike—I believe in the Torah; I believe in the Bible. My mom was Catholic until a friend introduced her to Islam, and I think my dad used to be Christian. So I'm really open-minded toward the views of other religions. I do try to find answers in the Qur'an—and I'm trying to learn Arabic so I can do that. But as a Muslim I'm not just going to read the Qur'an. I'm going in search of whatever I think is true in order to get a better understanding of my religion.

FAVORITE PLACE:

Niagara Falls.

FAVORITE MEAL:

Curry shrimp with red peppers, scallops, and fettuccine.

FAVORITE JOURNEY:

My trip to Aurora, Colorado.

GUILTY PLEASURE:

Staying up real late with a bag of chocolate Flipz watching *Ace Ventura: Pet Detective.*

MOST BOGUS MISCONCEPTION ABOUT MY BELIEFS:

That Islam and Middle Eastern culture are the same thing.

FAVORITE SLOGAN, SAYING, OR SONG LYRIC:

"You don't know what you've got until it's gone."

IF I FOUND A HUNDRED-DOLLAR BILL . . .

I'd spend it on shoes.

WHAT I MOST ADMIRE ABOUT MYSELF:

My ability to look past people's faults.

WHAT I LEAST ADMIRE ABOUT MYSELF:

I say it. Then think it.

Doubt is part of all religion. All the religious

FIVE PEOPLE (LIVING OR DEAD) I'D LOVE TO HANG OUT WITH:

My grandfather, whom I've never met; my best friend Amira, who lives in Denver, Colorado; my cousin Chelsea; my uncle Tappo; and maybe Shakespeare.

THE STRANGEST PLACE I EVER FOUND DIVINE POWER:

I think it was when I spoke with a family from Kosovo at a social gathering. The mother and I really vibed. We were surrounded by hundreds of people, and I couldn't even see or hear the other people, I was so focused on her. It seemed like I could feel her pain and understand each one of her struggles. And the strange thing was that this was before I even knew about the unfortunate events in her country.

sumanth

Sumanth Murthy
Hometown: Flushing, Queens, New York City
Age: 14
Gender: Male
School/Grade: Eighth Grade
Raised: Hindu
Currently: Hindu

Sumanth Murthy has lived exactly half of his life in the United States and half of his life in India. He moved to Flushing, Queens, in New York City, when he was seven, and this summer he'll visit Bangalore, India, where he was born. There are a lot of things about living in the United States that Sumanth loves— from basketball to Taco Bell—but he still makes certain that he keeps his religion and his heritage close. From a window in his family's apartment he can see the Hindu Center, where he is a frequent visitor. Just this morning he went there to help out and to pray. He says he prayed for his grandmother, for the health of his entire family, and for the New York Knicks.

religion: hinduism

Founder: Unknown

History: Hinduism was established in India, but the exact time is uncertain. 200 B.C. to 500 A.D. was a time of great flux, growth, and definition for Hinduism—the sacred laws were codified, the great temples began to be built, and myths and rituals were preserved in the Puranas (devotional texts).

Beliefs: Because there is no creed for Hinduism, it embraces a wide diversity of religious beliefs. Some Hindus worship Shiva (the god of destruction), others worship Vishnu (the life giver) or his incarnations, and others worship goddesses. There are many gods and goddesses and many manifestations of a single deity. Vishnu, for example, appears in ten forms, including a fish (Matsya), a tortoise (Kurma), and a boar (Varaha). Lakshmi is the wife of Vishnu and the goddess of fortune and beauty. Agni is the life force of nature. Indra is the sky god and god of war. Ganesa is one of the most popular gods because he is a symbol for good luck and wealth. There are a number of other gods and goddesses symbolizing the sun, moon, and stars. The concepts of reincarnation (the belief that individual souls survive death and are reborn in a different form) and karma are universal to most Hindus. Hindus also believe that the caste, or social class, people are born into depends upon their obedience in a former life.

Big Books: There are a number of sacred texts. Vedic literature is made up of the Rig-Veda (hymns), Sama-Veda (verses for chanting), Yajur-Veda (instruction for rituals), and Atharva-Veda (rites and spells). The Smriti (a list of practices that have been passed down orally) includes two epics, the *Ramayana* and *Mahabharata*, as well as the eighteen Puranas and textbooks on sacred law.

House of Worship: The temple or individual shrines at home.

Holidays: Di Wali is the autumn festival of lights, during which lanterns are lit to celebrate the gods' triumph over evil. Holi is a spring festival that celebrates the Hindu new year. Shivardtri is a holiday held in honor of Shiva— people fast and hold all-night vigils to honor him. Ganesa Chaturthi is the annual festival near the monsoon season in India, which lasts for ten days.

Do you still have ties to India?

I'm going back there this summer to visit my relatives and everybody. It's gonna be fun. This will be my third time back to where we're from, a place called Bangalore in the south of India.

Do you feel a special spiritual connection to India?

Yeah, I do. Whenever I go to India, I try to visit the temples that I haven't been to yet. Plus I get to hear everyone speaking my native language. This time I'm going to see more temples and pray and take pictures.

You also have a local temple at the Hindu Center near your home in New York. What do you do when you go there?

First I go inside and pray to all the gods. And then I see if the temple needs any volunteer work. I try to help often on weekends and especially on Mondays, when my friends come and we help out together. It feels good. I usually put milk out for the god Vishnu.

Why milk?

It's a way of worshiping the gods, of worshiping Vishnu. We're offering up our riches—milk, yogurt, honey, sugar, juice. We bathe a statue of Vishnu in milk to purify him, and then we make offerings of jewelry and flowers. We then get the milk to drink.

Because they hold certain animals sacred, many Hindus are vegetarian. Do you avoid eating meat?

Yeah. I'm a vegetarian. Everybody in my house is a vegetarian because we Hindus consider cows and some of the other animals to be gods. I'm used to not eating meat.

The spirit enlightens whom it chooseth.—Hindu proverb

SO YOU NEVER GO TO MCDONALD'S?

I go to McDonald's—I just eat the french fries. And I go to Taco Bell. I usually get Mexican pizza with beans instead of beef, and I get bean burritos and tostadas.

HINDUS GO TO TEMPLE SEVERAL TIMES A WEEK. DO YOU HAVE A RITUAL WHEN YOU GO?

Sure. Before I go in, I wash my hands. Then I walk around the temple and pray to all the gods. There are hundreds of Hindu gods and goddesses, so I start praying to all of them. Then I kneel down, bend over so my head is on the ground, put my hands together, and pray.

WHAT DO YOU PRAY FOR?

Goodness and health. I ask the gods for help in making everything go right and for all my family members to be okay. And I pray to try to keep a positive attitude.

WHAT ARE SOME OF THE BIG HINDU HOLIDAYS?

The biggest holiday is called Ganesa Chaturthi, which usually comes in August or in the first week of September. It's a ten-day festival in honor of Ganesa, the main god in our temple. Each day there's a different decoration for Ganesa. One day it's flowers; one day it's fruit; one day it's gold coins; one day it's nice jewels. On the last day there's a big procession with dancing and ceremonial dress.

WHY IS GANESA SUCH AN IMPORTANT GOD?

Ganesa is a remover of obstacles, and we pray to him because we don't want obstacles in our life. I think he's powerful because of his wisdom, which is explained in this story: Ganesa's parents had two sons, and his parents said that whichever son could travel around the world seven times first would be one of the most powerful gods. Ganesa's brother said, "I'll be

Philosophy is the talk on the cereal box. /

the first to go around the world and return," and left. Ganesa told his parents, "The world means nothing to me. You are my world." So he circled his parents seven times. They were amazed, and they made him the most powerful god.

MANY HINDUS PRACTICE YOGA AS A WAY TO UNITE WITH THE DIVINE. DO YOU DO YOGA?

Yes, I started four or five weeks ago. There's a swami (a Hindu holy man) who teaches a class every Sunday morning at the center. For the first hour and fifteen minutes we do yoga, and then for the last twenty minutes or so we do meditation. The swami teaches us to keep our bodies flexible and our minds free and to keep everything positive.

WHEN YOU MEDITATE, IS THERE SOMETHING THAT YOU TRY TO KEEP IN MIND TO HELP YOU FOCUS?

No, because the swami tells us to keep our minds empty. He says, "You are not this body; you are not this mind." He encourages us to calm down and make our pulses really slow. He encourages us to try not to think about anything while we meditate. The swami also tells us not to open our eyes because our minds follow our eyes.

WHAT IS THE SWAMI LIKE?

He's 109 years old. Every week he takes the subway from his apartment in Manhattan out to Queens. If you have any problems, you can go to his house and he will help heal you. He walks without anybody's help; he reads without glasses. In addition to meditation and yoga, he's taught me to avoid being ignorant and to try to be good, do good, and keep love with all.

AS YOU GET OLDER, HAVE YOU STARTED TO INCORPORATE THESE HINDU IDEAS INTO YOUR DAILY LIFE?

Every day, I'm learning more about the Hindu way of life. I feel like I'm getting used to it now, and I am thinking a lot about the swami's teachings. I'm learning more every day.

Religion is the smile on a dog.—Edie Brickell

FAVORITE PLACE:

India.

FAVORITE MEAL:

A sandwich.

FAVORITE JOURNEY:

Niagara Falls.

GUILTY PLEASURE:

Playing video games.

FAVORITE SLOGAN, SAYING, OR SONG LYRIC:

"Where there is a will, there is a way!"

IF I FOUND A HUNDRED-DOLLAR BILL . . .

It depends on the situation.

WHAT I MOST ADMIRE ABOUT MYSELF:

My honesty.

WHAT I LEAST ADMIRE ABOUT MYSELF:

I talk on the phone too much.

FIVE PEOPLE (LIVING OR DEAD) I'D LOVE TO HANG OUT WITH:

Gandhi; my grandparents; Babe Ruth, Albert Einstein; and Michael Jordan.

THE STRANGEST PLACE I EVER FOUND DIVINE POWER:

Within myself.

Stagnation is not a desirable state.

sumanth

Through struggle we develop strength.—*Papa Ramdas*

Miguel Mendoza gets excited when he talks about Buddhism: You can hear his mind racing, eager to relate the wisdom he's acquired and the revelations he's had. He was raised in a Catholic Filipino family and lives at home with his parents. His is the only room in the house that has an altar and a picture of the Dalai Lama. Miguel is a member of Students for a Free Tibet, a collegiate organization that supports Tibet's struggle for independence from China. He is also a careful Buddhist: He makes sure he refers to the Dalai Lama as His Holiness, the Fourteenth Dalai Lama. According to Miguel, Buddhism is the best thing that ever happened to him.

Miguel Mendoza
Hometown: Antioch, California
Age: 20
Gender: Male
School/Grade: Sophomore at Los Medanos College
Raised: Catholic
Currently: Buddhist

Founding figure: Siddhartha Gotama (the Buddha)

History: Founded in India around the fifth century A.D. as an offshoot of Hinduism. The young Buddha rejected some aspects of his native Hinduism—namely, the hierarchical class system—yet maintained many of the basic Hindu beliefs in reincarnation, nonviolence, and the renunciation of the material world.

Beliefs: The primary beliefs are that existence equals suffering and that humans can free themselves from this suffering and attain enlightenment, or nirvana, through meditation and selflessness, and the forsaking of the material world. The beliefs of Buddhism are distilled in the Four Noble Truths: that misery exists, that it comes from desire, that the desire or craving of pleasure can be overcome, and that this can be achieved if you follow a set path, called the Noble Eightfold Path. Buddhists believe in reincarnation, the idea that we have many lives rather than just one. Through many cycles of life, death, and rebirth, enlightenment is attained.

House of Worship: Temple.

Sects: Very early, Buddhism split into two main movements: Theravada Buddhism, which strictly follows early Buddhist scripture, and Mahayana Buddhism, which includes additional ideas. Theravada Buddhists believe there are seven buddhas in addition to Siddhartha Gotama. Mahayana Buddhists believe that there are unlimited buddhas, and that anyone can become a buddha by attaining enlightenment. In time, a number of different Buddhist strains, some based on geographical distinctions, developed from Mahayana, such as Zen, Japanese, and Tibetan.

The Way is not difficult; only there

You were raised by Catholic parents. How did you become a Buddhist?

For some reason I've always been inclined toward Buddhism and things from India. I first tried to meditate when I was eleven. Later I was told by a Tibetan friend that I might have been a lama (a Buddhist monk) in a past life. In my junior year of high school we learned about the Four Noble Truths and different aspects of Buddhism. My teacher spoke about it as if it were sketchy—she talked about nirvana like it was a wavy-gravy kind of thing, but I still found it really interesting. Since that time I've been studying different forms of Buddhism, reading different books, thinking, and meditating.

Were you confirmed in the church?

I was baptized, but I refused confirmation. By that time, when I was around thirteen or fourteen, I was getting more into my Buddhist studies. Catholicism held no spirituality for me, none at all. The Gospels meant nothing to me; they were just stories that I heard with my family on Sundays. Plus the people at the churches I went to were extremely materialistic—everyone was always looking at how everyone else was dressed. I mean, I can find God somewhere else.

Although you aren't a practicing Catholic anymore, do you see similarities between Christianity and Buddhism?

I find so many parallels between Jesus Christ and Lord Buddha. They both taught that we should love one another. Both had mothers who were supposedly virgins when they had them, and both experienced some sort of divine intervention in their births. Both Jesus and the Buddha spent their lives teaching compassion and love. Jesus didn't differentiate between a prostitute or a priest or a king, and Buddha did the same—he totally rejected the caste system of the dominant Brahmin society and the Indian upper class that he was born into. Both of them were rebels in a way—they didn't conform to the popular beliefs of their times. It sucks that so many people don't understand that there's so much that people of different religions can learn from one another.

What about Western culture? What can we learn from Buddhism?

His Holiness the Fourteenth Dalai Lama stated that westerners can benefit a lot from Buddhism by learning how to train their minds, learning how to meditate and to focus their thoughts. At the same time Buddhists can learn from the generosity of westerners and their humanitarian efforts.

When have you felt closest to your spirituality?

Zen Buddhism is a Japanese Buddhist tradition in which the path to enlightenment, or total awareness, is sought through moving beyond logical thought.

Well, when I was studying Zen Buddhism I couldn't understand the koans. [Koans are contradictory riddles given to Zen students to solve. Example: If you meet someone in the street who has reached the truth, you may neither walk past him in silence nor speaking. How then should you meet him?] I didn't get them, which is kind of the point, and I had this realization that sometimes you can't describe an experience with words. I had a tiny *satori* (a glimpse of enlightenment).

Where were you when you had this satori?

I was at work at the Chevron station. I was taking out the garbage, and for some reason, I'm always in a Zen-like state when I'm taking out the garbage. The garbage may stink, but I don't attach myself to the smell. I don't grasp on to it. In that state I'm extremely aware, so I was thinking about the concepts I'd been reading about, like the idea of impermanence, leads to suffering. I loved the elation, the feeling that I had just realized something, but then I thought, If I grasp on to this elation, how can I expand my mind? This is just a glimpse—if I hold on to this wonderful feeling, it will totally limit me. So I let it go.

Those who want the fewest things

who is the dalai lama?

His Holiness the Dalai Lama is the recognized leader of Tibetan Buddhism (a mixture of traditional Buddhism and an ancient Tibetan form of nature worship) and the spiritual leader of Tibet. The Dalai Lama, who has, according to Tibetan Buddhism, reached enlightenment, was born as Lhamo Dhondrub in 1935 in a small village in Tibet. At the age of two, he was recognized by Tibetan scholars and monks as the fourteenth reincarnation of the Dalai Lama (as well as the reincarnation of Avalokitesvara, the Buddha of Compassion) and began preparing for his role as Tibetan Buddhism's highest-ranking holy man. He has devoted his life to learning, teaching, and writing about Buddhism as well as working toward the political and spiritual liberation of his homeland. The Dalai Lama was forced to flee Tibet in 1959 when it was seized by the Chinese government. He has not set foot in his native country since that time but continues to work toward the freedom of his homeland from India, where he now lives, and abroad. Many groups support this struggle, including Students for a Free Tibet.

ONE OF THE MAIN TEACHINGS OF BUDDHISM IS TO SHOW COMPASSION AT ALL TIMES. HOW DO YOU EXERCISE COMPASSION IN YOUR LIFE?

Well, when someone's trying to wrong me, like at school or when I'm working at Chevron, I try to just give them the benefit of the doubt and try to understand what they're going through.

Buddhism requires a still, meditative mind. Do you meditate?

Yes. Sometimes I'll just sit for three minutes to get focused, and other times I'll go for an hour or so. At first I was like, "Relax, dammit! Clear your mind!" but in *The Tibetan Book of Living and Dying*, the author, Sogyal Rinpoche, talks about how your posture should be that of a mountain: No matter what clouds swirl around it, it's just there, steady and still. Your mind should be without grasping; you should let thoughts pass as if they were clouds in the sky.

Do you have a mantra—or a chant—that you use during meditation?

Mani Padme means "the jewel in the lotus" and <u>om</u> and <u>hum</u> are words with special supernatural power.

Yes: "Om Mani Padme Hum." It's a common one in Tibetan Buddhism, and it evokes Avalokitesvara, who is the Buddha of Compassion.

With a few more years of college ahead of you, how do you plan to further your Buddhist studies?

I want to be a monk, so I'm scouring the Internet for a Buddhist monastery to join after I finish school. There's only so much you can do by visiting a center or reading books. I want to expand my knowledge and learn from real Buddhist masters.

What do your friends say about your beliefs?

Most of them are so cool about it. I talk to them about Buddhism, and they dig it. But my conservative Catholic friends hate it. They think I'm just bullshitting myself and trying to be all cool. They think I'm a poser. They don't understand. Every day of my life right now I feel so much better because I'm walking in pure mindfulness. And they don't want to see that. So I'll pray for them—that's all I can do.

miguel on karma bead bracelets:

They've become so trendy! I hate that. It's like someone who's not Christian wearing a cross. They're prayer beads—for reciting mantras. If people are truly spiritual about wearing them, that's different. I'm all for it. But I don't like that this whole consumer culture is eating up Buddhism and Hinduism as if they were just trends.

miguel on his prized possessions:

I have a tin box that holds a picture of His Holiness the Fourteenth Dalai Lama, some Tibetan incense, and a picture of the green Tara, a female deity of compassion. It's a very maternal, positive feminine image to meditate on. I carry the box with me everywhere.

FAVORITE PLACE:

Walden West Science Camp, Saratoga, California.

FAVORITE MEAL:

Anything my mom or grandma cooks.

FAVORITE JOURNEY:

One summer a whole bunch of my friends and I decided to go to a local haunted bridge. When we got there, there was this really freaky-looking guy walking in the middle of nowhere at four o'clock in the morning. We all got scared, busted a U-turn, and drove to San Francisco. On the way there we heard "My Sharona," and we all started to dance in the car like the freaks we were. It was just such carefree bliss. It was drizzling, and we decided to walk the length of the Golden Gate Bridge at sunrise.

GUILTY PLEASURE:

That I actually like 'N Sync's song "Bye Bye Bye." What can I say? It's catchy.

MOST BOGUS MISCONCEPTION ABOUT MY BELIEFS:

That it revolves around a fat, smiling Chinese man or that "it's just a phase."

FAVORITE SLOGAN, SAYING, OR SONG LYRIC:

FREE TIBET!!!

There are many paths to enlightenment.

IF I FOUND A HUNDRED-DOLLAR BILL . . .

I would give $50 to my mom for spending money, and the other $50 I'd probably spend on Tibetan clothes and Buddhist-ritual items.

WHAT I MOST ADMIRE ABOUT MYSELF:

My pseudo-Tibetan/Raver Kandy Kid sense of style.

WHAT I LEAST ADMIRE ABOUT MYSELF:

My inability to be fully compassionate.

FIVE PEOPLE (LIVING OR DEAD) I'D LOVE TO HANG OUT WITH:

Lord Buddha; Jesus Christ; Lao Tzu, an ancient Chinese philosopher; Jack Kerouac; and James Michael Strazinsky, the creator of the TV show *Babylon 5*.

STRANGEST PLACE I EVER FOUND DIVINE POWER:

At a Santa Rosa, California, hospital. My mother had a cerebral aneurysm. I was still Catholic then, and I prayed that if she lived, I would never question the existence of God again. Three days later she woke up from her coma. Family members from all over the United States were there praying, and we all rejoiced when she awoke. Even though I'm no longer Catholic, I have never questioned the existence of God since that day.

Nili Chernikoff
Hometown: Ewing, New Jersey
Age: 19
Gender: Female
School/Grade: Freshman at Bard College
Major: Photography
Raised: Conservative Jew
Currently: Conservative Jew

Every Friday night Nili Chernikoff invites a bunch of friends over to her college dorm room for dinner. As the sun sets, Nili lights candles and says a prayer over them, blesses the food and thanks God for it and starts serving dinner. Friday evening marks the beginning of the Jewish Sabbath, the chosen day of rest. Nili, whose father is a rabbi, keeps kosher and also keeps what is called Shomer Shabbos, so from Friday at sundown to Saturday at sundown she avoids driving (except to go to synagogue), tries to not use electrical appliances (including the phone), and does no work—she won't even pick up a pencil. Even though most of her dinner guests aren't Jewish, they help Nili celebrate her Judaism. "The Sabbath," she says, "is supposed to be different from every other day, and having friends over to dinner helps make it special."

religion: judaism

Founder: Abraham

History: Around 1800 B.C. in Ur of the Chaldees (an ancient land in Mesopotamia), the prophet Abraham began questioning the reigning polytheism (religions based on the belief in more than one god) and asserting that there was only one God. As a result the people of Ur persecuted him and forced him to flee, and he and his followers sought refuge in what Jews believe to be the promised land, Canaan.

Beliefs: Judaism is centered on the belief in one God, who is the creator and ruler of the world. According to Jewish scripture, God revealed his laws to Moses on Mount Sinai, and Jews are expected to keep these 613 commandments, which govern every area of daily life from diet to civil law. Jews believe that they are God's chosen people and that they are to reflect the character of God in their daily lives. They await the coming of a messiah, or savior, who will redeem their suffering and restore them to their promised land.

Big Books: The Torah, which shares the five books of Moses with the Christian Bible.

House of Worship: Synagogue.

Holidays: The major Jewish holidays, called high holidays, are Yom Kippur (the day of atonement, which is a time of fasting and repentance), and Rosh Hashanah, which is the Jewish new year and is celebrated as the anniversary of creation.

Other Sects: Judaism includes varying levels of observance and tradition: from Orthodox, which is the strictest and most traditional in its observance, to Conservative, to Reformed, the observance of which is more assimilated to the demands of the modern world. There are Hasidic Jews, who are ultra-Orthodox, and Kabbalists, who study an ancient form of mystical Judaism.

All souls are one. Each is a spark of the original soul

Your father is a rabbi—which means he's a religious teacher and leader as well as an example for the community. There's a lot of pressure in that. Did that pressure carry over to you as you were growing up?

A lot of times when a parent is a visible leader, the whole family is visible, so there's a lot of pressure to set a good example. I remember when I was little, like five years old, I was running around in synagogue and some older lady came up to me and said that I was the rabbi's daughter and the rabbi's daughter wasn't supposed to do such things.

Plus you always had to go to synagogue.

No. My parents never forced me to go to synagogue—at least not since I was in high school. If I didn't want to go, no one made me. On the whole I liked going, and I wanted to be there.

What do you like about going?

The atmosphere and the sense of camaraderie. You're all there with a common goal: to worship. I wouldn't say it's

> Because the name of God is sacred, devout Jews don't write it out. Instead they refer to the creator as "G-d."

the most exciting experience every time you're there, but there's a spiritual sense you get when you're there, and you're all sharing in a service. Everybody prays for different reasons, everybody has connections to G-d for different reasons, but when you're in the synagogue for services, you're sharing in a common spiritual experience.

and this soul is inherent in all souls.—Hasidic saying

You've been practicing Judaism your whole life. Did you ever doubt your beliefs?

No. Judaism encourages people to ask questions and seek answers, so whenever I encountered something in my religion that I wasn't completely sure of, I asked about it. I don't believe that we are meant to have all of the answers. We can't always understand why certain things happen in the world, and expecting an answer to drop out of the sky isn't realistic. At some point pure and simple faith with no qualifications has to come into play. It's this type of faith that I have relied upon when I'm at a loss for why certain things occur.

Judaism—from ultra-orthodox to ultra-liberal

Judaism recognizes various levels of observance and includes many different lifestyles. There are three main branches of Judaism: Reformed, Conservative, and Orthodox. The most common observance in the United States is Reformed. Reformed Jews don't follow many of traditional Judaism's, strict rules and commonly attend services only on important holidays. Conservative Jews typically go to synagogue more frequently and observe many of the traditional laws pertaining to diet and the observance of the Sabbath [holy day], but have adapted some of them to suit modern-day life. Orthodox Jews strive to uphold all the traditional observances—from not handling money on the Sabbath to maintaining a strict kosher diet and sometimes keeping certain kinds of traditional dress.

Peace is important, for

BEING BROUGHT UP AS A CONSERVATIVE JEW, YOU WERE EXPECTED TO FOLLOW A LOT OF RULES AND RESTRICTIONS. DID YOU EVER REBEL AGAINST YOUR PARENTS?

Sure. There were moments when I was little when I would want to draw and color pictures on the Sabbath, or I would want to go out with my friends on a Saturday. But ultimately, as I grew older and learned more about my religion, my beliefs and practices began to stem more from myself than from my parents. At this point I no longer do or don't do things because someone told me to; I do it for myself and for my own beliefs.

YOU WENT FROM A JEWISH DAY SCHOOL TO A SECULAR HIGH SCHOOL. WAS IT HARD TO KEEP KOSHER AND KEEP OBSERVING THE SABBATH AS THE DAY OF REST?

All through high school people would ask me, "Couldn't you just cheat for one Friday and come out, anyway?" But if you grow up doing certain things, it's not a challenge to keep doing them. I'm not going to say that I was never sad if I missed a dance at school on a Friday night, but it was never such a great decision to make. I just knew it wasn't something that I did.

WHAT ARE THE BENEFITS OF STAYING HOME FRIDAY NIGHTS FOR THE SABBATH?

Shabbos is the day of rest—that's what it's supposed to be—and I've always felt that there are a lot of things I get out of that. I mean, I get to really rest on Friday nights and Saturdays. Sometimes it's hard because I can't do any homework on a Saturday, so that leaves me just with Sunday, but at the same time it's nice because I'm actually able to rest and not feel guilty that I'm not doing my work. The Sabbath is a time to rejuvenate and get back energy for the next week—and that's what Judaism intended it to be.

IS THE SABBATH A MORE SPIRITUAL TIME FOR YOU?

Obviously if you're resting and you're not busy thinking about the whirlwind of the life you're living, you have time to think spiritually.

God's name is Peace.—Midrash Tahama

IS KEEPING UP WITH YOUR SPIRITUAL TRADITIONS MORE DIFFICULT IN COLLEGE THAN IT WAS AT HOME?

It is difficult. I came to Bard College because it was intellectually alive and they had a good photography program, but it's not the most spiritually inclined place. They don't have kosher food at the school, and they don't have services on campus, but I'm making it work. I drive to a synagogue nearby and get my food at a supermarket that's not that far away. I guess Bard has a very liberal atmosphere, and it seems like a lot of people think that organized religion isn't really compatible with that type of thinking. I can only speak for myself, but spirituality is such an important part of my life, I can't imagine it not being a part of my college experience.

THE LAWS OF KEEPING KOSHER ARE VERY INVOLVED, AND DIFFERENT PEOPLE INTERPRET THEM IN DIFFERENT WAYS. AT THE MOST BASIC LEVEL, HOW WOULD YOU DESCRIBE WHAT MAKES FOOD KOSHER?

Well, it's really complex and it does vary for different people, but in general food is kosher when the production of it has been supervised by a rabbi, who makes sure that it's prepared according to kosher law.

IS THERE A SPIRITUAL VALUE TO KEEPING KOSHER?

I just feel that it's the right way for me to live. Eating can be a really mundane thing that you never really think about, but when you keep kosher, every time you eat, you're thinking about it, and it connects you back to your religion. That's especially true for me, being at Bard and not having kosher food. It's more of a decision now. I think when you live in a Jewish community where everyone's keeping kosher, you don't really think about it so much. I've had to explain a lot more about how I keep kosher, why I keep kosher, than I ever did before. Back home, my family kept kosher, so I kept kosher. Now it's a choice I make.

Man's love of God is identical

IT MUST BE DIFFICULT TO FULLY UNDERSTAND THE SPIRITUAL SIGNIFICANCE OF ALL THE VARIOUS TRADITIONS. WHEN YOUR FRIENDS ASK ABOUT CERTAIN PRACTICES, WHAT DO YOU SAY?

I don't know everything there is to know about my religion. I think you could study Judaism your entire life and never know everything there is to know. Sometimes people ask me why I'm doing a certain practice, and I don't always know the answer. It's special to me. It makes me feel special and it gives a structure and purpose to my life. Judaism comes into play in every little part of my life, in all the decisions that I make. I'm still learning. I don't know why every single practice that I do is meaningful, but I know that it makes me feel good.

WHEN HAVE YOU FELT THE MOST SPIRITUAL?

Probably when I was in Israel two summers ago. Suddenly I was in these places that I'd been learning about; they weren't photographs, they were actual places. I know that when I prayed there, it was definitely different for me than praying at home. We hiked all over the country and would sometimes get up at three in the morning to hike to the top of a mountain. And we would stand on the top of this big mountain and pray as the sun was rising. A beautiful sunrise, that made us appreciate being here on earth for another day. So we were standing at the top and we were praying and singing and dancing and I was just . . . I don't know . . . happy.

IS THERE A JUDAIC SAYING THAT'S ESPECIALLY MEANINGFUL TO YOU?

I can't come up with the exact translation, but it's something like, "If I am not for myself, who will be for me? If I'm only for myself, what am I? And if not now, when?" You have to look out for yourself, but if you're only looking out for yourself, you're not really living a fulfilling life.

nili on marriage:

Right now my feeling is that I'll only marry another Jew. Some people think that's prejudice, but religion is such a big part of my life, and I couldn't imagine sharing my life with someone I couldn't share my religion with. I just know that that would be too difficult for me.

nili on keeping the faith:

I'm teaching religious school for the first time this year. I'm teaching sixth graders, and they are preparing for their bar and bat mitzvahs [a traditional coming-of-age ritual that Jewish boys and girls celebrate when they turn thirteen; it requires the study of the Torah and Hebrew and marks their entry into Jewish adulthood]. I've been preparing my class and teaching them a lot of the prayers. One morning, on the fifth anniversary of my own bat mitzvah, they led the service and I read the Torah. I felt a real connection to G-d, and it was great because I got to see these kids that I've been teaching experience that same kind of special connection that I've been trying to share with them. It was very special to me.

Reading the Torah at your bat mitzvah is symbolic of accepting the duties of a Jew and becoming a participating member of the Jewish community.

As long as there is life,

FAVORITE PLACE:

Jerusalem, Israel.

FAVORITE MEAL:

Pizza and ice cream.

FAVORITE JOURNEY:

A really great dream I had, which took me to exactly the place I wanted to be at that time.

GUILTY PLEASURE:

Watching hours of TV when I'm home on breaks from school.

MOST BOGUS MISCONCEPTION ABOUT MY BELIEFS:

That's a hard one. I guess I just think that so many misconceptions could be cleared up if people would ask questions about practices and beliefs they don't understand, instead of forming opinions that have no foundation.

FAVORITE SLOGAN, SAYING, OR SONG LYRIC:

"Don't worry, be happy." —Bobby McFerrin.

IF I FOUND A HUNDRED-DOLLAR BILL . . .

I'd wonder if there were hidden cameras waiting to see if I picked it up, so I'd probably leave it there.

I MOST ADMIRE ABOUT MYSELF:

I'm a good leader, and I enjoy helping other people.

I LEAST ADMIRE ABOUT MYSELF:

I'm often too quick to argue with other people, and I usually feel badly about it afterwards.

FIVE PEOPLE (LIVING OR DEAD) I'D LOVE TO HANG OUT WITH:

Jean M. Auel, a historical fiction author; Yitzhak Rabin, former Prime Minister of Israel, who was assassinated in 1995; Montaigne, a great philosopher; and my grandfathers on both sides, whom I never had the opportunity to meet.

STRANGEST PLACE I EVER FOUND DIVINE POWER:

This is going to sound really silly, but when I was in fourth grade all I wanted was to win this art poster contest. I prayed every night for weeks that I would win it, and about a month later my art teacher told me that I'd won. I don't know if that really falls under "divine power," but I didn't question G-d's ability after that!

That's me in the spotlight /

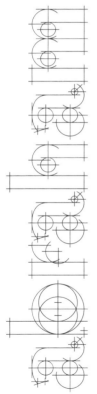

Rabbi Jeffrey Salkin is the head rabbi at the Central Synagogue in Port Washington, New York. He has written several books, including Putting God on the Guest List: How to Reclaim the Spiritual Meaning of Your Child's Bar or Bat Mitzvah. *Here's what he had to say about Abraham's rebellious years.*

There's a wonderful legend that every Jewish child knows: When Abraham was thirteen, he smashed his father's idols (which are images worshiped as gods) and by doing that became the first monotheist (the first believer in only one God). Abraham's father was an idol maker, and this action marked the first time Abraham rebelled and began to think for himself. He took many steps in this direction. Later, Abraham saw people coming into his father's store all the time and buying idols that had been built a few days before, when the customers themselves were seventy-five or eighty years old. And he said, "How can you worship something that's younger than you?" The search for the absolute, for that which is ancient, for that which is more ancient than anything else, brought Abraham to the idea of one God. And so Western religion began with a teenager breaking away from the false religion of his parents. It's a very powerful idea. If it were not for those acts of rebellion, then Judaism would not have come into existence.

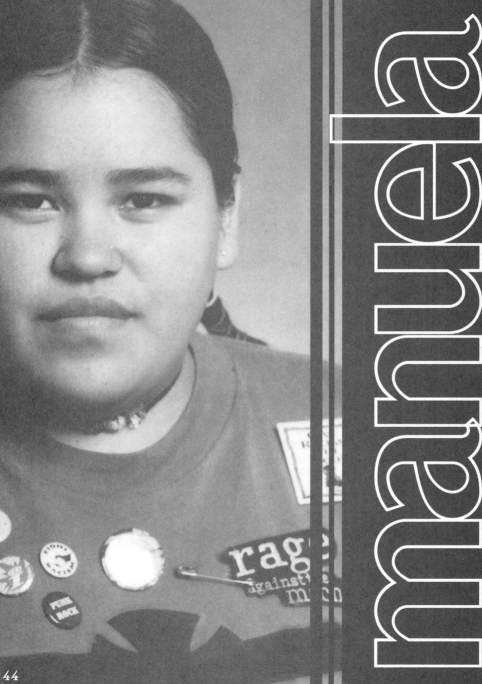

manuela

Manuela Perez
Hometown: Wimauma, Florida
Age: 16
Gender: Female
School/Grade: Sophomore in High School
Raised: Catholic
Currently: Unaffiliated/New Age

Manuela Perez would be the first to tell you that spirituality and religion are not one and the same. In fact, she'd say that religion is often spirituality's worst enemy. Having rejected the Catholic faith she was raised in, Manuela finds her answers elsewhere—she takes a little wisdom from her reading, a little guidance from the New Age movement, and a little solace in the stars above.

YOU HAVE A PRETTY ECLECTIC BELIEF SYSTEM. HOW WOULD YOU DESCRIBE YOURSELF IN TERMS OF SPIRITUALITY?

I believe in the so-called New Age movement, and I feel that I'm part of it. For me, that means living conscious of the power of life and the presence of meaning in everything. I believe in the paranormal and other ideas that are not so easily seen or believed. To me, spirituality is being aware of your true self and affecting everything with the piercing beauty of the truth that resides in you (and in everyone). I am living. I still learn many things each day, and I am not afraid to see things from my own point of view and experience. I can read Wiccan and Buddhist literature, and I can read nihilist rantings—this is how I create my beliefs, my personal way of living and being. I also believe that "God" is everything. Therefore, we are God. I truly believe this—even though it's very hard to explain to others.

> *The New Age movement is a combination of spiritual, social, and political elements that aim for spiritual transformation. Yoga, holistic healing, tarot, and martial arts are used to find an understanding of human divinity and the unity of all creations.*

YOU MENTIONED THE NEW AGE MOVEMENT. WHAT, TO YOU, IS THE MOVEMENT ALL ABOUT?

To me, it's about the beginning of the end of the old ways of thinking and living. New Age embraces everything. It's a free way of thinking and living. It's also the most eclectic and different form of spiritual expression I can imagine. That's what I'm searching for, and that's what I've found in the New Age movement: a different way of thinking and living from what I've been taught. It's the greatest movement I have ever encountered.

You need a busload of

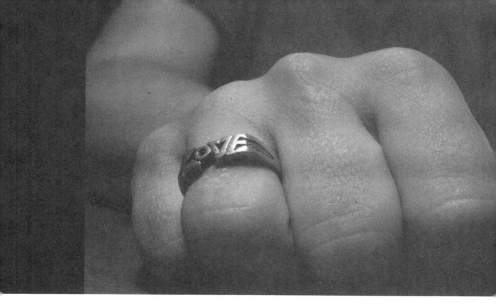

How do these beliefs figure into your life at 16?

I still struggle with the stereotype of what you're supposed to be at the age of 16, which—from what I've seen and heard—is not much. I don't try to act differently, but I feel different. I'm not sure if that's a good thing, but it's very hard thinking about the meaning of everything when you have to get to second period.

What would you rather be thinking about?

I want to be thinking about how I can change the world. That sounds so naive, but I really do. I seriously want to be out there doing something. I want to help people out on a grand scale. I try to communicate with others and tell them that, but it's very difficult.

What kinds of changes do you want to focus on?

The injustice that minorities face in this country and in other countries as well. Poverty and the gap between the poor and the rich, especially the

faith to get by.—Lou Reed

ruling class, which is usually white. And indifference—just indifference to everything. I know it's hard caring about the world when you've got to deal with the mundane, but it's so important. I've been known to be very dogmatic about this stuff, but I don't want to come across that way. I just feel very strongly about my issues and what I believe.

DOES THIS ATTITUDE STEM FROM YOUR SPIRITUAL BELIEFS?

I think just seeing the world spiritually causes you to want to help as much as possible. Help others see how truly beautiful it all is. How pointless murder and control are. How great humans can be and how we need to collectively reach a goal for living. I still believe that we all have something that connects us and nothing can break that. So why aren't we helping each other? Why are we fighting? What is distracting us?

People don't come to church for preachments,

Where do you feel most at peace spiritually?

I feel most at peace in nature, at the beach, especially at night. Just looking up at the stars, stargazing. That's where I feel the basic power of being human and being a part of the beauty of it all. Under all the hurt and decay and the problems, there's just a basic beauty that's been there all along. I think there's a spiritual void within, and I don't think that it can be filled by a television set or a movie or whatever else. I think there are forces that run the world without us noticing. When you sit outside and just ponder nature and watch nature happen, you can really get in touch with it. But modern life has taken that away—it has removed us further from nature.

What's your take on drinking and smoking?

I feel that they're a hindrance and that they're targeted to young people in order to trap them into a cycle of need. And that's just completely wrong. I try to tell that to everyone, but people don't understand how buying a pack of cigarettes helps some huge company to continue dominating the country. Everything's interconnected, and people don't want to see that.

Is that a Straight-Edge philosophy?

The Straight Edge movement is based on the idea that drugs, alcohol, tobacco, and promiscuous sex prevent a person from being physically and psychologically independent. Recent interpretations of the Straight Edge philosophy also include a vegan diet and political activism.

Yeah. I really like the punk rock, Straight Edge, hard-core scene. I like the politics and activism of it all. Straight Edge is a lot about taking the power over yourself into your hands and not giving that power to other people. Not letting people entice you with things that are addictive, like drugs, alcohol, and tobacco.

of course, but to daydream about God.—Kurt Vonnegut, Jr.

What kinds of spiritual reading do you do?

I love philosophy; I read it every day, and that influences me a lot. I like Thoreau, who was very spiritual, and Jean-Paul Sartre. Good philosophy is so personal; it's very deep and very true. I can't even begin to explain to you how philosophy completely changed my life in just a matter of months.

What was your life like before that change?

I had a lot of childhood problems—problems with identity. I don't fit the mold for what most people would say being Mexican is, and down here where I live, that's a big issue. I live in a Mexican barrio, where most of the girls my age are either out of school and planning to get married or they're already married with kids. Still, I used to participate a lot in school and in the life that was going on around me. I had a lot of friends, but within a year—when I was between 14 and 15—I changed completely. I lost who I was, the feelings that I thought I knew, the future that I thought I was going to have, the friends that I thought I had, the family connections I thought I had. I truly felt that life would never be the same again after that period. I let myself fall in a deep and difficult depression. I no longer believed in anything. Everything was dead to me. But even as I felt the cold reality of isolation and the heat of hatred, I felt that somehow this period was going to be the catalyst for a new beginning, a new life, if you will. I was broken and naked. Lost, but on the track to whatever I was supposed to find.

And what did you find?

This incredible book, *Conversations with God*, by Neale Donald Walsch. It was the book that not only changed my life but really defined all the spiritual feelings and thoughts that I've had my whole life. It put what I felt was true about life into words. I found it on one of my weekly escapes to the library. The back flap simply read something like, "What if you could ask God anything that you have ever wanted? Well, Neale Donald Walsch had such a conversation with God, and here is what God had to say." I read the book,

Do not seek to follow in the footsteps

> *According to* Conversations with God, *Neale Donald Walsch had become so depressed about his life that he dashed out an angry letter to God. To his surprise, he got answers to his questions about humanity and his own life. The book chronicles his conversations with God.*

and I became utterly enlightened. Needless to say, this book was the Pandora's box to my rediscovery of self through knowledge and writings.

THESE BELIEFS ARE A FAR CRY FROM THE CATHOLIC BELIEFS YOU LEARNED GROWING UP. HOW DO YOU FEEL ABOUT CATHOLICISM NOW?

There were always "church ladies" who visited us migrants in our camps and taught their beliefs to us. As a child, I believed every word they said. I remember the fear of hearing about Armageddon for the first time. It's not that I don't respect Christians, but I have now placed myself as far as possible from Christianity.

SO HOW HAS YOUR LIFE'S PATH CHANGED FROM WHAT IT WAS ORIGINALLY?

My old path was basically doing what my parents wanted me to—going to college and getting a degree and getting a job and helping them out. I do want to go to college, and even though I'd do anything to help my parents, I wouldn't be very happy following that expected path. I'm still searching for my own path. I think everyone is.

manuela

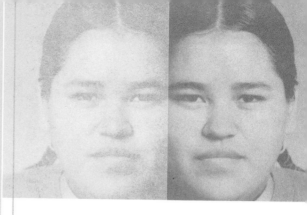

FAVORITE PLACE:

The beach on a clear, starry night with calm waters and a full moon.

FAVORITE MEAL:

Pizza. Anytime, all the time.

FAVORITE JOURNEY:

Dreams are my favorite journeys; also the never-ending, lifelong journey to find meaning and truth.

GUILTY PLEASURE:

Junk food, sitcoms, pop culture.

MOST BOGUS MISCONCEPTION ABOUT MY BELIEFS:

That my beliefs aren't valid because they're new or different. The biggest misconception about what I believe is that it's just a phase because I'm 16 and rebellious. But my beliefs are here to stay!

Beauty is eternity gazing at

FAVORITE SLOGAN, SAYING, OR SONG LYRIC:

So many! "I never let my schooling interfere with my education"—Mark Twain. Also: "Sometimes just waking is surreal"—A.F.I. (a band)

IF I FOUND A HUNDRED-DOLLAR BILL . . .

I would use it to organize a protest.

HOW I'D REALLY SPEND IT:

I could use some comfortable pants, more music, and activist literature.

I MOST ADMIRE ABOUT MYSELF:

My individuality.

I LEAST ADMIRE ABOUT MYSELF:

My inability to deal with other human beings. I want to help humanity, but sometimes I can't stand them!

FIVE PEOPLE (LIVING OR DEAD) I'D LOVE TO HANG OUT WITH:

Trent Reznor of Nine Inch Nails; Zach de la Rocha of Rage Against the Machine; Jim Morrison of The Doors; Aleister Crowley, the self-proclaimed Beast; and Buddha.

STRANGEST PLACE I EVER FOUND DIVINE POWER:

I have honestly found God in the worst emotions possible. Good feelings are generally thought to bring that feeling of grandness (God), but I find God in hatred, ugliness, pain, misery, despair, and Nine Inch Nails's music! I feel that if you could find God in the most extreme opposite emotions, then you have a much greater understanding of God.

itself in a mirror.—Kahlil Gibran

Marcos Lewis
Age: 19
Hometown: San José, California
Gender: Male
School/Grade: Freshman at the School of Visual Arts,
New York City
Major: Illustration
Raised: Nonreligious
Currently: Baha'i

Marcos Lewis takes a seat at a Starbucks on Third Avenue in Manhattan, sits up straight, and begins nibbling on his oatmeal cookie. He's wearing squarish glasses, a Nappy T-shirt, a black knit hat with an Asian symbol on it, and a big smile on his face. He says the symbol is Japanese for the New York Yankees. Marcos is nineteen and a relative newcomer to New York. Like everything he does, his decision to go to college in New York had a lot to do with a choice he made on his seventeenth birthday, when he took it upon himself to become a member of the Baha'i faith. "I knew I wouldn't be alone in New York," he says, "because I knew there was a big Baha'i community here."

religion: baha'i

Founder: Baha'u'allah

History: In 1863 Baha'u'allah (a name that translates to "Glory of God") proclaimed himself to be a manifestation of God, the last in the line of divine manifestations, including Buddha, Jesus Christ, and Muhammad. He professed to be a prophet sent by God to the world to abolish racial, ethnic, and gender inequality and to establish a universal religion.

Beliefs: Baha'is are known for their teachings of racial harmony, equality of the sexes, modesty, temperance, and self-education, and for embracing the similarities of the world's religions. They believe in working toward universal faith, government, and education.

Rituals: Although there are no official Baha'i rituals or services of worship, Baha'is gather to read the scriptures (see *Big Books* below) for cultural and social events and programs. Young believers often do a year of service, either spreading the faith or assisting existing Baha'i communities around the world.

Big Books: The writings of the Bab, Baha'u'llah, and Abd ol-Baha complement but also supersede the Torah, the New Testament, and the Qur'an.

Holidays: Baha'is partake in an annual fast, a nineteen-day period of self-sacrifice, reflection, and atonement. At the end of the fasting period they celebrate their new year (Naw Ruz) with a feast and festival.

THE BAHA'I FAITH IS PRETTY OBSCURE. HOW DID YOU FIRST FIND OUT ABOUT IT?

Through friends. When I was fourteen, I was in one or two dance groups in the San José area and a friend of mine invited me to a performance, what Baha'is call Workshop. It was put on by a Baha'i youth group that spreads

Teachers open the door,

the word of the Baha'i faith through the arts. So I invited my parents, and we all went.

WELL, YOU MUST HAVE LIKED IT.

What really attracted me was the step dance. It's a lot of hand clapping and rhythm-of-the-body kind of thing. The Workshop had a huge step dance, and because I was into dance, that kind of hooked me into the group. I stayed in the group for about three years, talking to people and picking up the general Baha'i philosophy. It just made a lot of sense to me.

WHAT MADE SENSE TO YOU?

Many of the Baha'i principles are pretty much the same values I'd grown up with. For instance, racial unity, self-education, humility, and the equality of men and women—that's how my parents taught me. So Baha'i was kind of like finding people with like ideals.

BUT YOUR PARENTS WEREN'T BAHA'IS?

No. My dad was a fundamentalist Christian in his first two years of college and my mom wasn't Baha'i, either, but now she is.

YOU SAID THE BAHA'I WORKSHOPS USE THE ARTS TO SPREAD THE WORD ABOUT THEIR RELIGION. WHY?

Because the arts are kind of a universal thing that everyone can relate to. Though not everyone has the same vocabulary or the same language, not everyone can read, everyone likes art, and everyone is creative in some way. I've been interested in drawing and painting for a while, but the Baha'i teachings are what really got me jazzed to go to art school.

IS THERE A MESSAGE TO THE ART?

The arts are a tool through which to spread the teachings of Baha'u'allah, but they can be expanded to whatever your imagination can come up with as long as it's beneficial to the faith. In Workshop every dance has a purpose. A dance's purpose can be to show the unity of the group, or to show the Baha'i solutions to racism, or to show the situation of poverty in America. The art is always used for some purpose.

WHICH DANCES MEAN THE MOST TO YOU?

The Martyr's dance symbolizes the martyrs who, in the early years of the faith, went against the social grain to spread the Baha'i teachings and ended up dying for their beliefs. The dance shows the martyrs spreading the faith, their persecution, and their ascension into heaven. Doing the dance means a lot to me, not only because of the message but also because of the unity of the group when it's being performed. When you're making those loud sounds and you're stepping on the floor and smacking your hands until they're red, the audience realizes that your message must be important. So for straight impact and drama, I like that one.

WHEN YOU WERE IN HIGH SCHOOL, DID YOU TALK ABOUT YOUR BELIEFS TO YOUR CLASSMATES?

When it came to talking about my faith at school, there was always the fear, "What's everyone gonna think?" It was tough sometimes because there were only four Baha'is in our high school, and when you've got a fairly controversial religion that few adults know about, it can add to that fear.

WHAT ABOUT WITH YOUR FRIENDS?

My friends say, "Wow, Marcos, why are you so happy?" And I say, "Because God woke me up today," and they're like [he furrows his brow in skepticism], "Really?" In the beginning I was afraid of that skepticism. But I'm stronger now, and I can speak about it with confidence.

He that does good for good's sake,

marcos on conflict:

Baha'u'allah talks about trying not to be the cause of anyone's sorrow or grief. So even if someone's in my face, like when I'm getting on the subway and someone bumps into me and says, "What the hell's your problem!" I try to say, "Okay, I'm sorry, excuse me." By handling it this way, I'm stopping the conflict and refusing to let it escalate. And maybe if I'm nice to that person, they might realize they're not being very cool.

WHEN YOU FINALLY DECIDED TO BECOME BAHA'I, YOU SIGNED A CARD DECLARING YOUR FAITH. HOW DOES THAT WORK?

For Baha'is, the age of maturity is fifteen, so from fifteen on you can sign your declaration card because you're considered a mature adult. I signed mine on my seventeenth birthday. Signing the card is a personal thing.

DID YOU RECEIVE ANY TRAINING OR PREPARATION?

The first law that Baha'u'allah talks about is to be a seeker, and the first law of the seeker is the independent investigation of truth. You're supposed to seek out the truth and find it for yourself. In my case, I went to Workshop, I liked it, and then it was my responsibility to get more information, to read books and talk to people to find out if Baha'i was for me.

marcos on music:

I listen to hip-hop. You know The Roots? I listen to them a lot, and they sometimes curse in their songs, but they don't curse a whole lot, and it's mostly for emphasis. So stuff like that doesn't even faze me. But when it comes to the other stuff where every other word is an expletive and the message is making money and having sex . . . that doesn't interest me at all. So I'm not going to listen to it.

HOW DID YOU KNOW THE TIME WAS RIGHT?

The card was sitting on my desk for a good two months, and something told me, "This is serious. You can't play around with this. If you're going to sign this card, you have to be able to take on the responsibility. So for a while I kept asking myself, "Are you ready for this?" Then on my seventeenth birthday something told me, "You have to sign it. Only good things can come from that." It was a strange feeling of relief because I was still anxious about what might come but excited, too.

WHAT KINDS OF THINGS WERE YOU ANXIOUS ABOUT?

I was worried about what people would say and whether I'd be able to convince them that this was right for me. At the time, it mattered to me because, like everyone else in our society, I formulated my idea of myself based on what other people told me, instead of formulating it on what my mission under God is. I didn't like getting into discussions about the Baha'i faith at the time, because I was so worried that I'd say something wrong.

If a man wishes to be sure of the road he treads on,

It was kind of selfish in a way because I had this idea that I, Marcos, could topple this entire religious movement just by saying something wrong.

HOW HAS YOUR DAY-TO-DAY LIFE CHANGED SINCE YOU SIGNED THE CARD?

It has changed 180 degrees. On the outside not much has changed. I still smile a lot, make folks laugh, and give people the utmost respect. But on the inside, I have a better outlook on life. Since I became a Baha'i and declared my faith, my smiles and laughs are more genuine. There was a point in my life when every act I did was to gain acceptance and fit in. Now everything I do is for God, and instead of fitting in I am raising up. I am not perfect, but I am better than I was, and I want to help the world get better.

WHAT DO YOU MEDITATE ON?

We have a chant, "Allah u Abha," which means "God is most glorious," and we have to say that ninety-five times a day. So that's kind of like my meditation. Instead of just rolling out of bed and brushing my teeth, I try to commune with God in the morning, so I might just try to center myself or, if I have a certain difficulty, I might meditate on that. Or I just focus on the good things in life and on just being thankful.

BAHA'IS ARE ENCOURAGED TO AVOID NEGATIVE INFLU-ENCES THAT ENCOURAGE WORLDLINESS OR EMOTIONAL BEHAVIOR LIKE CURSING. HOW DO YOU DECIDE WHAT'S OKAY TO WATCH, READ, OR LISTEN TO?

We're taught to find things out for ourselves, but there are some things you don't have to experience in order to analyze. Sex is a good example. You don't have to watch a porn film to know what it's all about. You're supposed to be curious when you're looking for knowledge, but you don't have to experience everything to know what's right for you.

he must close his eyes and walk in the dark.—John of the Cross

Baha'is are encouraged to avoid getting involved in politics, because politicians are not following in the way of God. And sex. We're not supposed to have sex outside of marriage. I'm celibate. I wasn't a big stud in high school, so it doesn't bother me so much.

fasting

Technically, fasting means a total or partial abstinence from food—usually for religious purposes. But the significance of the act differs from one religion to the next. It can be a function of self-denial, a way to atone for sins, a way to purify the body or to simply help shift focus from the body to the mind and spirit, because the person fasting has less energy and more time to reflect. Fasting is also often considered a way of showing devotion by foregoing personal comforts and practicing self-denial.

In some tribal religions fasting is a preparation for a ceremony or initiation. In Judaism and Christianity fasting can be a way to repent for sins or to honor or emulate the past; Christians restrict their diets during Lent to honor and imitate the forty-day fast Jesus Christ endured before he was crucified. Fasting is especially common around religious holidays: Muslims fast from dawn to dusk of every day in the month of Ramadan, and Jews fast during Yom Kippur.

I have had the experience of being gripped by something that is

What are the big Baha'i holidays?

There's Ayamiha, which is five days of celebration and relaxation before we start the Nineteen-Day Fast, which is when we abstain from food and drink from sunup to sundown, almost like Ramadan [the Islamic month of fasting]. Then right after that is the Baha'i new year, which occurs in March.

Fasting has different meanings in different religions. What does it mean to you, as a Baha'i?

When we fast, we're supposed to take time to reflect on the past year. I pray a lot during that time because it helps me deal with the hunger pains. I pray for assistance to help me through the day, and it makes a difference. Fasting slows you down—you move slower because you don't have the energy to run back and forth for this, that, and the other thing. You're supposed to go slow because you're supposed to be thinking about things and communing with God and putting everything in place.

Does your faith give you hopefulness about the future?

Sure, because there's somewhere to look for knowledge about what's ahead of me. There are actual books; actual scriptures that say, in the future, such and such will happen. So I always have a sense of what might come.

Does that include an afterlife?

Baha'is believe that, in this life, we're fostering and gathering spiritual knowledge so that once we pass on to the next life we'll be inclined to do the best that we can. Baha'is don't have the conception of heaven and hell as places. It's not like if you're spiritually undeveloped you're going to end up in some big boiling pot—you're just going to be further away from God because you don't have that knowledge. You're going to have a chance to get that knowledge and love and reverence, it's just going to take more time.

FAVORITE PLACE:

As long as I am around positive, bright people who are hungry for knowledge, any place will do. It sounds cheesy but it's true.

FAVORITE MEAL:

Chicken (doesn't matter what kind), peas and rice, string beans, and mac n' cheese.

FAVORITE JOURNEY:

The discovery of new and enlightening things.

MOST BOGUS MISCONCEPTION ABOUT MY BELIEFS:

My own belief that, in my lifetime, I will get it all down and be a perfect Baha'i.

IF I FOUND A HUNDRED-DOLLAR BILL . . .

After taking it to the authorities and waiting two or three weeks for someone to claim it, I would spend half on food and entertainment and give the other half to the local Baha'i fund.

Unless a person is happy,

WHAT I MOST ADMIRE ABOUT MYSELF:

That I have learned the value of education.

WHAT I LEAST ADMIRE ABOUT MYSELF:

That I don't always ask for help (divine or otherwise) when I need it.

FIVE PEOPLE (LIVING OR DEAD) I'D LOVE TO HANG OUT WITH:

My older brother Roberto; my brothas from a different motha, Justin and Ryan Portillo, who introduced me to the faith; Gina, my Baha'i home girl from New York; and finally Chenoah, my ace from Cali.

THE STRANGEST PLACE I HAVE EVER FOUND DIVINE POWER:

Inside me.

he cannot bestow happiness on others.—Ramana Maharshi

britt

Britt Bonner
Age: 19
Hometown: Conyers, Georgia
Gender: Male
School/Grade: Sophomore at Emory University
Major: History
Raised: Evangelical Christian
Currently: Evangelical Christian

Britt Bonner describes himself as a spirit-filled Christian. That means that he'll do anything— he'll sing and lift his hands in worship and even shout and dance—when the spirit moves him. He'll play guitar in the Christian rock band he started called Throne. But all that prayer and public jubilation doesn't mean nearly as much to Britt as the quiet time he spends in prayer or the friendship he has with God. Here, he talks about his faith in his own words.

religion: christianity

Founding Figure: Jesus Christ

History: Christianity is founded on the worship of Jesus Christ, who, according to Christian belief, was born, died, and rose from the dead in fulfillment of the prophecies of the Old Testament. After his death Jesus's teachings were spread by his most devoted followers, the apostles, who worked to build the foundations of the Christian church.

Beliefs: The main principle of Christianity is the acceptance of Jesus as the messiah, the savior of humankind from death and sin. All Christians—from Roman Catholics to Baptists, from Evangelists to Protestants—believe that God sent his only son, Jesus Christ, to live on earth to spread the word of God, to be crucified, and to ascend into heaven. They believe that in accepting his own crucifixion, Jesus accepted the sins of his followers, giving them absolution, while his rise into heaven promised them the chance at eternal life.

Big Books: The Bible, which includes the Ten Commandments, a code of behavior that Christians are supposed to follow.

House of Worship: Church.

Holidays: Christmas marks the birth of Christ, though many historians dispute the actual date of December 25. The forty days prior to Easter, which are called Lent, symbolize the torment and temptation Christ experienced before his betrayal and crucifixion. Easter week is the holiest of Christian holidays: Good Friday marks the death of Christ; Easter Sunday celebrates his ascension into heaven.

Other Sects: There are hundreds of different sects and varying interpretations of Christianity. The main divisions are between Roman Catholicism, Eastern Orthodox, and Protestantism, which itself includes scores of different traditions and religious organizations.

The Lord is with me;

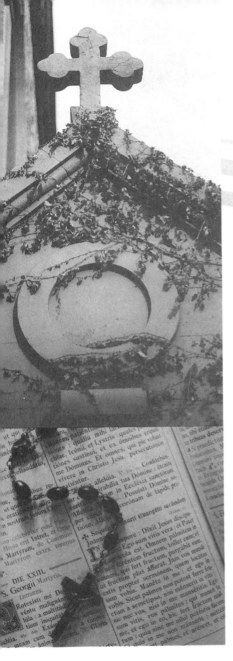

People ask if I'm a religious person, and I say, "No, I'm not very religious, but I am very spiritual." I don't think you have to wear a suit and a tie and do certain things to reach God and to find spirituality in your life. I often use the word Churchianity because to a lot of people that's what Christianity has become. They come to church and sit on a pew; they go through their acts of religion for the week and they think they're getting closer to God. But to me, spirituality isn't a list of dos and don'ts. The focus is on having a relationship with Jesus Christ and letting him sort of put the dos and don'ts into your heart.

When you have a relationship with Jesus, you don't need marijuana to feel good on a Friday night. You don't need sexual games and relationships because you're no longer searching. You have fulfillment. In high school I sensed a lot of hopelessness in my peers who were involved in the whole drug scene, the party scene. I had a lot of girl friends (meaning girl *friends*) who would get with a guy and lose their virginity, and then after a while the relationship would fall apart. I just sensed such a spiritual dryness around me . . . a hunger.

So some friends and I started the band Throne. Initially the music was nothing to be proud of. The purpose was to reach our peers with our message. We started playing every Thursday night at our church, which is a very

what is evangelism?

Evangelical Christianity emphasizes a personal relationship with God and the authority of the Bible. Evangelical Christians believe that each person needs to be spiritually reborn and come to know Christ, which often happens through a conversion experience.

nontraditional, nondenominational church in a warehouse building beside a gym. In the first week we had about eighteen people come out, but a year later there were close to two hundred coming on a consistent basis. We'd do about thirty or forty minutes of music, and then I'd normally give a real brief talk to the kids. I'd say, "This is what has happened in my life; I've come to know God, and I have a personal relationship with Him." I would offer that to them, and inevitably we'd have fifty or so who would respond by saying they wanted that, too. So many kids are so hungry, but they're not really aware of where that hunger is coming from. They're going through stuff at home, they're dealing with relationships, they're trying to fit in at school—but deep inside they're crying out for something. I think that when we were created, we were made with a spiritual void, and through the course of life (especially in our teenage years) we're on a search for fulfillment. And I believe that until you have a relationship with God, you cannot fill that void.

I was raised knowing God—through my parents, who are ministers, and my grandfather (Archbishop Earl Paulk), and through the church—so I always had a bit of that fulfillment. But there came a point, when I was about thirteen or fourteen, when I realized that I had to get to know God

Seek good, not evil,

britt on God and fun:

There's a misconception that Christians are boring. In reality, on Thursday nights, walking into our church is like walking into a nightclub. We've got the lights and the heavy-rock music. It's not about going into a boring setting to find God. God's an exciting God, and we want to show that.

britt on parties:

In high school, because of the band, everybody knew who I was and what I was all about. So I had a responsibility to live up to—because I was preaching my values every Thursday night, and everybody knew it. When I did go to parties, it was a big thing to try to get me to hold a beer. People would say, "Just put this beer in your hand," or, "Britt, hold my cigarette for a few minutes." They just wanted to see me compromise so it would make them feel better. But that's not what I'm about.

for myself. It was a spiritual awakening—when I learned that I needed to spend time with God every day. I started dedicating thirty minutes every day to sitting in my room and coming to know Jesus. I realize now that I need that for myself.

To be honest with you, if I hadn't made a commitment to God and really started seeking and finding that quiet place with Him, there's no telling where I would be today. Because I'm no different from anyone else. I'm a young person. I have the same feelings and emotions and desires as the next guy, and I can't say I've never been tempted to go down the wrong path. The thing that I really try to emphasize and live out in my personal life is that being close to God is a daily relationship. It's like having a best friend. If you never talk to that friend, then you don't really know him. So I talk to God every day. Some days it just happens in my car. I'll be driving down the road, and I'll just feel that urge. It's like a little tug on my heart sometimes. It's sort of like God calling.

holy place

music by Britt Bonner, Mark Harris, and Dale Drummond

© 2000 *Throne* music

I COME INTO YOUR PRESENCE LORD,
    I'M RUNNING TO YOUR THRONE
I RUSHED BEYOND THE GATE OF PRAISE,
    JUST TO WORSHIP YOU ALONE
TAKE ME INTO YOUR HOLY PLACE,
    I HUMBLY BOW BEFORE YOUR THRONE
    I CAN'T MAKE IT ON MY OWN
THE SACRIFICE CAME THROUGH YOUR SON,
    WHO SITS AT YOUR RIGHT HAND
THE CLOSER I GET TO YOUR FACE,
    MY KNEES CAN HARDLY STAND

Faith is often strengthened right at the

FAVORITE PLACE:

On a stage leading others in God's presence.

FAVORITE MEAL:

Filet mignon cooked medium rare with a baked potato and a slice of white chocolate cheesecake for dessert—plus a Dr Pepper to drink.

FAVORITE JOURNEY:

To Pensacola, Florida, with my family, to visit the beach and a church that is experiencing a great revival. The trip was great, and we were all touched by God at the revival.

GUILTY PLEASURE:

Skipping school.

place of disappointment. —Rodney McBride

MOST BOGUS MISCONCEPTION ABOUT MY BELIEFS:

That Christianity is based on a set of rules and regulations. I believe it's all about a relationship with Jesus Christ!

FAVORITE SLOGAN, SAYING, OR SONG LYRIC:

"Love your neighbor as yourself," from the Bible.

IF I FOUND A HUNDRED-DOLLAR BILL . . .

I would use it to feed the hungry.

WHAT I'D REALLY DO:

I'd put it toward buying the new guitar I've been wanting.

WHAT I MOST ADMIRE ABOUT MYSELF:

That I genuinely care about people and about seeing them find their purpose in life.

WHAT I LEAST ADMIRE ABOUT MYSELF:

That I'm a procrastinator! I try not to be, but it's nearly impossible. I can't remember ever doing a college paper any other time than the night before (even the fifteen-pagers!).

FIVE PEOPLE (LIVING OR DEAD) I'D LOVE TO HANG OUT WITH:

I'd invite Jesus Christ; Kathryn Kuhlman, a great faith healer; Smith Wigglesworth, a great man of God; T. L. Osborn, a well-known evangelist; and Billy Graham, another very well-known evangelist.

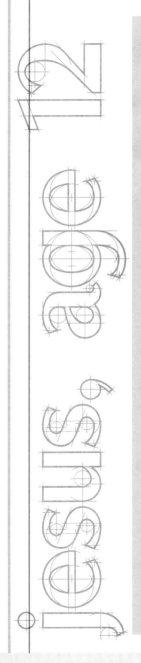
Jesus, age 12

Bishop Chilton Knudsen is the Episcopal Church's bishop of the state of Maine. Here's how she interprets what the Bible says Jesus might have been like as a teenager.

According to the Bible, when Jesus was about 12 years old, he and his family went up to a festival in Jerusalem. After his parents had started back home, they discovered that Jesus wasn't with them. So they returned to Jerusalem, and eventually they found him in the temple, sitting among the Jewish scholars, listening and asking questions on an adult level. Everyone who heard him was amazed at the nature of his insights. But his parents were upset. They asked him why he'd left them to worry where he'd gone. He replied, "Did you not know that I need to be about my father's business and in my father's house?" By saying this, Jesus is acknowledging that his life has some purpose apart from his parents. When he says, "Did you not know I needed to be in my father's house?" he's obviously not referring to his earthly father, Joseph. As the son of God, he is acknowledging a greater affiliation to God. It's very clear that the father's house that he had been growing up in, which was the home of a carpenter in the town of Nazareth, was no longer the house in which he was called to dwell. But at the end of the story Jesus does go back with Mary and Joseph (his parents) to Nazareth. The Bible says, ". . . and Jesus grew in both body and in wisdom, gaining favor with God and man." So while he's had an excursion into adulthood, he knows that he is not yet ready to be fully adult. He's made a claim upon his selfhood, he's experienced freedom, and he's separated himself from his parents, but he knows he needs a few more years within the family unit.

like Jesus to a child. —George Michael

Lunar Dragon (alias)
Age: 17
Gender: Male
School/Grade: High School Senior
Raised: Nonreligious
Currently: Kabbalist

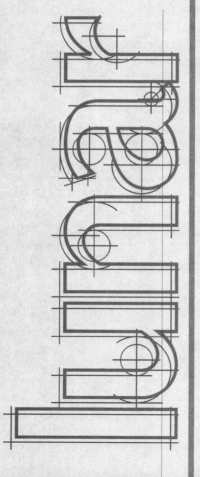

Lunar Dragon prefers to be anonymous (that's why you won't see his picture on any of these pages). Just think of him as a high school senior who's good with a computer and has a penchant for studying a two-thousand-year-old mystical form of Judaism called Kabbalah. Studying the Kabbalah requires an active and open mind, and Lunar may be the perfect candidate. He's got a thirsty brain and a diverse spiritual background: His father is from a Conservative Jewish family and his mother is a Catholic.

religion: kabbalah

Founder: Unknown. Some believe the practice of Kabbalah dates back to the time of Adam, who, according to the Old Testament, was the first man created by God.

History: Kabbalah is a sect of Judaism that solidified in thirteenth-century Spain and France, though sects date back to the first century A.D. Kabbalah means "to receive." It is based on an oral tradition passed down through the generations by ancient Jewish mystics. Though Kabbalah has traditionally been a discipline passed from one Jewish scholar or rabbi to another or taught in secret, a number of new books have introduced it to a more mainstream audience. In modern times many people practice Kabbalah without keeping Jewish laws and celebrating Jewish holidays.

Mysticism is the belief that union with the divine can be achieved through intuition, faith, or ecstasy. A mystic is one who seeks that personal and intense interaction with the divine.

Beliefs: Kabbalists believe that by analyzing and interpreting the Torah, they can unlock the secrets of the universe and its creation. Through rituals, astrology, special techniques, and careful analysis of the mystical meaning of the letters of the Hebrew alphabet, Kabbalists strive to see heavenly visions. Ecstatic fits are often accepted as part of that journey.

Big Books: The Torah and the Zohar, a seven-hundred-year-old text on Jewish mysticism.

There is no grief in

Kabbalah has, historically, been very underground. Why was it so secretive, and how did individuals come to practice it?

Kabbalah was always extremely esoteric. Originally if you weren't an exceptional student of the Torah (and a male over 40 years old), you couldn't learn much of the Kabbalah. The really magical Kabbalah groups were even more secretive. To avoid misunderstandings and even persecution, these groups met in secret, and inductees didn't find the lodges (groups of Kabbalists); the lodges found them. Now society's open-mindedness and willingness to share information has made it possible to use all sorts of resources to find information on Kabbalah. At one time mystics were afraid to even distribute a small pamphlet; now they have Web pages.

How did you discover Kabbalah?

In the strangest and most roundabout way. I needed money to get my girlfriend a nice good-bye gift. I was moving, and we were never going to see each other again. The problem was that as usual, I was broke. I didn't have enough money to get her that $80 ring at the jewelers, so I bought myself a book called *Magick for Beginners*, by J. H. Brennan, a Kabbalist author. It had a spell called the "$100-bill trick," and I was very desperate. As it turned out, I enjoyed the sections on metaphysical theory and basic mystical grounds more than the rituals promising the power. That's how my interest was sparked. I never did the spell, by the way, but I was eventually able to save up and get her the ring.

Traditionally Kabbalah was meant to be taught by a master (a rabbi) to a disciple. Do you study with a rabbi?

No, but there are several books on the subject, although some effect is lost because Kabbalah is an oral tradition. Plus, there are no Kabbalistic rabbis that I know of in my town. If it weren't for the modern methods of information (books, the Internet, etc.), I couldn't know Kabbalah until I reached 40 years old, found a rabbi willing to teach me, and went through all of mainstream Judaism first.

rituals

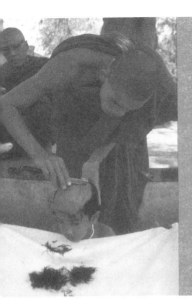

Rituals are religious ceremonies performed according to a set pattern of words, movements, and symbolic actions. Their purpose is to help the faithful get in touch with a divine power, sometimes by re-creating essential religious myths. Christian baptisms imitate Christ's own baptism by water, and Buddhist monks shave their heads to reenact the Buddha's renunciation of the material world. Other rituals mark important milestones: from birth to adulthood, marriage to death. Baptisms, circumcisions, wedding ceremonies, confirmations, bar mitzvahs, and other rites of passage are events that almost everyone in a specific faith experiences, binding them to the other members of their religion through symbolism and tradition.

AND AS YOU MENTIONED, YOU WOULD HAVE HAD TO HAVE BEEN A MALE. TRADITIONALLY WERE WOMEN ALLOWED TO PARTICIPATE IN KABBALISTIC ACTIVITIES?

Orthodox Judaism teaches that men are supposed to take the responsibility for studying religion and women are supposed to take responsibility for the home.

Kabbalah was primarily practiced by Orthodox Jews, so no. Thankfully, though, due to current social standards, many prominent Western mystics and magicians are women—some even have their own lodges.

YOUR MOTHER IS A FORMER CATHOLIC. WHY IS MYSTICAL JUDAISM MORE COMPELLING TO YOU THAN CATHOLICISM?

Modern Christianity (as distinguished from the purer, ancient kind founded by Jesus, who many believe was himself a Kabbalist) doesn't focus

When a sage is angry,

on the mystical and to me doesn't go deep enough into the cosmology of the world. Brennan, the author of the book I mentioned, states that a well-performed mass is one of the most amazing rituals, with the most profound effects he has ever witnessed. But more often than not, the priest runs through the physical ritual without full knowledge about the inner workings or true meanings. Then the practice has no effect.

Do you meditate, pray, or connect in some other way?

Mostly I meditate and try to live a Kabbalist's life by finding examples of the universe's glory in everything around me.

When do you feel closest to what you consider to be a divine power?

Meditating, admiring a tree, looking out on vast expanses of nature, and listening to people talking about their lives.

How do the teachings of the Kabbalah inform your morality?

Kabbalah teaches basically what many religions teach: "Do unto others as you would have them do unto you." The only difference between religions on this point is the logic they use to enforce it. Kabbalah is persuasive

how do you spell kabbalah?

Since Kabbalah is an ancient mystical tradition that was largely passed on and recorded orally and in secret, there are many differing spellings for it. Kabbalah comes from the Hebrew root word gabb_l_h, which means "tradition," or literally "to hand down." Kabbalah may be the most widely accepted spelling, but it isn't the only one. Here are a few others: Qabalah, Cabala, Qaballah, Qabala, Kaballah.

because it's mystical. We are one. "Do unto others as you would have them do unto you" because on some level, you're doing it to yourself, anyway. All souls are pure emanations from God and should be treated with respect—all of them. Including oneself. This helps my self-esteem also. Another thing Kabbalah stresses is charity, especially the Jewish practice of giving 10 percent of your income to charity. If I *had* an income, I might be more active in this tradition.

According to this form of numerology, each Hebrew letter has a number value, so when you add the numbers of the letters that make up words, you can discover connections and symbols. Numbers and letters are often a code through which to find secrets of the universe.

WHAT DOES NUMEROLOGY —THE STUDY OF NUMBERS AND THEIR HIDDEN SIGNIFICANCE—HAVE TO DO WITH KABBALAH?

Numerology is another way of analyzing the symbolism of the Torah and the world around us. In practice, the numbers link symbols in ritual workings in a similar manner. Each Hebrew letter has a number value, so you can imagine the possibilities.

ONE OF YOUR PARENTS IS A CATHOLIC, AND THE OTHER IS JEWISH. HAS YOUR RELIGIOUS BACKGROUND OPENED YOUR MIND TO THE POSSIBILITIES OF YOUR OWN SPIRITUALITY?

Absolutely. I'm fortunate to have an eclectic belief system because do you know what you find at the bottom of all religions? One religion. I merely simplify the confusing elements of each to lift my consciousness higher.

ARE YOUR PARENTS SUPPORTIVE OF YOUR KABBALISTIC STUDIES?

They're skeptical, and they don't believe in the same things I do, but they pass me a book every now and again and don't impede my process.

Men cling to the

lunar dragon on the commonality of religions:

On a mystical level, all religions are saying the same thing, just with a different vocabulary. As Rabbi David Cooper states in _Mystical Kabbalah_, a Hindu mystic, Buddhist mystic, Jewish mystic, Christian mystic, and Native American mystic can all sit down and talk without arguing and, through a simple matter of proper analysis, reconcile all of their religions.

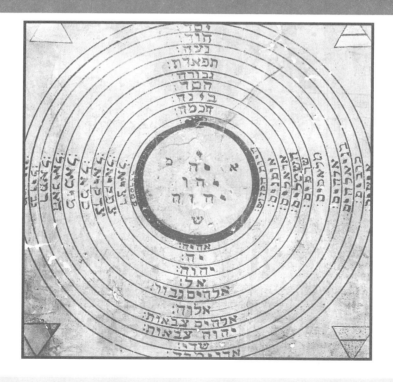

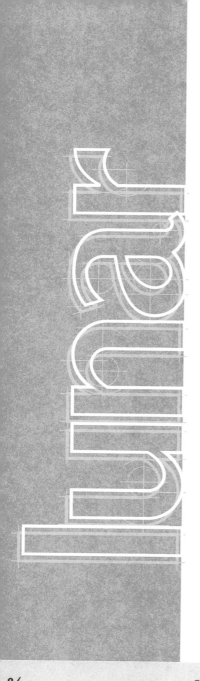

FAVORITE PLACE:

I've moved so often and found beauty in so many things that I can only say Earth and dare not to be more specific.

FAVORITE MEAL:

Stuffed artichoke.

FAVORITE JOURNEY:

Philosophical answer: life. Otherwise: long road trips with any destination.

MOST BOGUS MISCONCEPTION ABOUT MY BELIEFS:

You name it: that we're Satan worshippers, evokers of demons, that we try to bypass the laws of physical reality, and so on. The Western bias against anything with mysticism or magic brings about a whole spectrum of misconceptions, mostly stemming from the movies. Mysticism and magic focus on physics, but physics of the higher planes. We can't break any physical laws; we can only perceive and influence things that go by a different set of laws altogether.

FAVORITE SLOGAN, SAYING, OR SONG LYRIC:

It changes frequently. Usually I look toward works by Ralph Waldo Emerson, Henry Thoreau, and J. R. R. Tolkien.

If one contemplates the things in mystical

IF I FOUND A HUNDRED-DOLLAR BILL . . .

I'd give it to charity.

WHAT I'D REALLY DO:

I'd spend it on my girlfriend.

WHAT I MOST ADMIRE ABOUT MYSELF:

My innate awareness that I am not aware of much of which I could be aware.

WHAT I LEAST ADMIRE ABOUT MYSELF:

Arrogance is the worst enemy of a mystic. I've got some of it; that's extremely bad, and I'm working on it daily.

FIVE PEOPLE (LIVING OR DEAD) I'D LOVE TO HANG OUT WITH:

J. R. R. Tolkien; J. H. Brennan; and John Michael Greer, all good authors on the occult; Rabbi David Cooper, good Kabbalah author; and Moses, if he would be kind enough to come down.

STRANGEST PLACE I EVER FOUND DIVINE POWER:

In the eyes of my enemies.

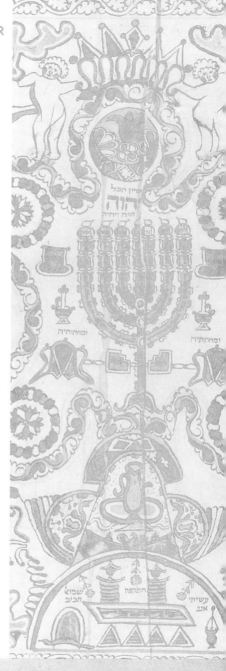

Karma Lama
Hometown: Shady, New York
Age: 13
Gender: Female
School/Grade: Seventh Grade
Raised: Buddhist
Currently: Buddhist

People expect great things from someone named Karma Lama. The Sanskrit word karma means "action," as in every action causes an effect, and it's a major principle of reincarnation. Lama is a name for a Buddhist monk. The thirteen-year-old girl who goes by that pretty, powerful name says that karma also means "star," but that doesn't prevent her friends from making lots of annoying karma jokes.

Karma Lama was born in Nepal to Tibetan parents. Her father (pictured right) is a Rinpoche, or a high-ranking lama, who fled his homeland of Tibet (which was occupied by the Chinese army in 1950) to Nepal and later moved to upstate New York—where he helped to build a monastery of Tibetan Buddhism. It took him and others fifteen years to build the Karma Triyana Dharmachakra, and now, most evenings, Karma goes there for *chenrizig*, the daily Buddhist teachings meant to cultivate loving kindness and compassion. While Karma admits she doesn't always

want to go, and she doesn't always understand everything that's being said, she usually does her best.

"The truth is," Karma explains, "I can't read Tibetan very well, so I just read the English. And I don't always know what everything means." But even when her mother makes her go to the temple, Karma knows that's the place she wants to be. "It feels nice when I'm there because I'm experiencing the teachings with everyone else, though sometimes I just like practicing alone."

This summer Karma and her two younger sisters are going to begin learning Tibetan. "Last summer we went to Tibet, and all these people would come up to us and start speaking Tibetan. It was really embarrassing—we are Tibetan, but we can't speak it, and we can't really read it." She also hopes that she can begin to deepen her practice of Buddhism over the summer months. "I'm always keeping up with academic stuff, and it's really hard to fit in religion, so I don't usually find time to practice. But I want to. This summer I'm going to try to do more." And according to Karma, nobody is a better mentor than her dad. "Sometimes if he has the time, my father and I get together, and I practice my Buddhist teachings," she says. "Or we get together and read. I like being with him—it's fun studying with other people, but it's different when you're with your dad. Especially since he's a lama (a Buddhist holy man). I'll ask him questions, and he's the best person to talk

Water which is too pure has no fish.—Ts'ai Ken T'an

to. He explains everything so well. He teaches me a lot." But it's not always easy being the Rinpoche's daughter.

"Sometimes," Karma admits, "it's so embarrassing. People will point to something written in Tibetan and ask, 'What does that say?' and I don't know. So they'll say, 'But you are Rinpoche's daughter.' Well, I think I know that by now." But despite the misconceptions people have about what a lama's daughter is supposed to be, Karma knows she's lucky to live in such close proximity to a holy man, even if she often takes it for granted. "I'm in such a good position, but I don't really take advantage of it," she explains. "When we were in Tibet, we'd see monks praying. They were so religiously connected, and I didn't understand that connection at all. I feel horrible about that."

karma on her sacred place:

We've got this really large yard, and there's this little rock patio where I like to sit and watch the mountains and everything. It's the best place to be when I'm trying to meditate. It sounds kind of corny, but that's the truth.

karma on her spiritual future:

I don't know what's in store for me in the future. I might have friends who believe in some other god, and I might find that I can relate to that more. We'll see. If that happens, I hope my dad understands—he's a really understanding person. But then again, because he has such an important role in Buddhism, it might be hard to tell him.

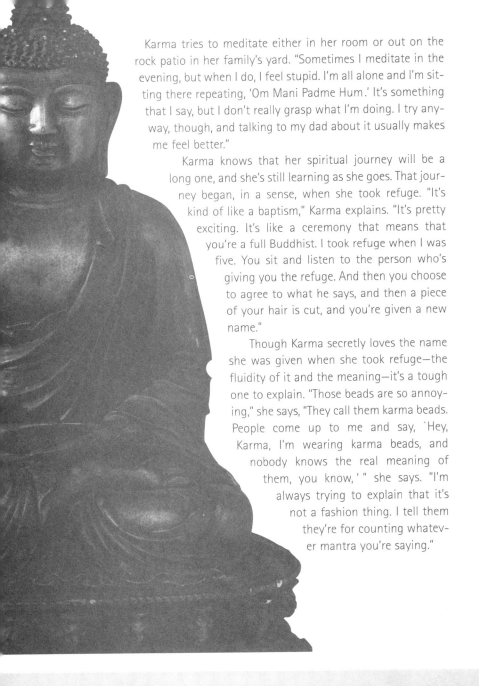

Karma tries to meditate either in her room or out on the rock patio in her family's yard. "Sometimes I meditate in the evening, but when I do, I feel stupid. I'm all alone and I'm sitting there repeating, 'Om Mani Padme Hum.' It's something that I say, but I don't really grasp what I'm doing. I try anyway, though, and talking to my dad about it usually makes me feel better."

Karma knows that her spiritual journey will be a long one, and she's still learning as she goes. That journey began, in a sense, when she took refuge. "It's kind of like a baptism," Karma explains. "It's pretty exciting. It's like a ceremony that means that you're a full Buddhist. I took refuge when I was five. You sit and listen to the person who's giving you the refuge. And then you choose to agree to what he says, and then a piece of your hair is cut, and you're given a new name."

Though Karma secretly loves the name she was given when she took refuge—the fluidity of it and the meaning—it's a tough one to explain. "Those beads are so annoying," she says, "They call them karma beads. People come up to me and say, `Hey, Karma, I'm wearing karma beads, and nobody knows the real meaning of them, you know,' " she says. "I'm always trying to explain that it's not a fashion thing. I tell them they're for counting whatever mantra you're saying."

In walking, just walk. In sitting, just sit.

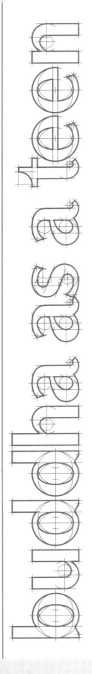
buddha as a teen

Robert Thurman is an expert on Tibetan Buddhism, a professor of religion at Columbia University, and an author of several books, including Essential Buddhism *and* Inner Revolution: Life, Liberty, and the Pursuit of Real Happiness. *Here's what he said about the importance of youth in Buddhism:*

Buddha was kind of a rebel, a revolutionary. He was told by his elders, "This is how it is," or, "You can't really fix this or do that"—but he didn't agree with them. And that's how he became Buddha—by not agreeing with those things. So the idea of breaking away from many kinds of conventions is very much a part of the Buddhist tradition.

So in Buddhism, wisdom is represented as youth cutting through the conventional wisdom that has been handed down but isn't really true. It is looking at things freshly and seeing that sometimes a dogma that has been handed down may not be very useful and cutting through it. It's a venerable tradition in Buddhism.

FAVORITE PLACE:
My relatives' house in Nepal.

FAVORITE MEAL:
Sushi.

FAVORITE JOURNEY:
My trip to Tibet.

When you understand one thing through

GUILTY PLEASURE:

Watching soap operas.

MOST BOGUS MISCONCEPTION ABOUT MY BELIEFS:

That all people who are Buddhists are monks and that everyone is always meditating and bald.

FAVORITE SLOGAN, SAYING, OR SONG LYRIC:

"It makes me ill to see you give love and attention at his will" —'N Sync

IF I FOUND A HUNDRED-DOLLAR BILL . . .

I'd put it in the bank for college.

WHAT I MOST ADMIRE ABOUT MYSELF:

My tolerance.

WHAT I LEAST ADMIRE ABOUT MYSELF:

I'm not good with managing my time.

FIVE PEOPLE (LIVING OR DEAD) I'D LOVE TO HANG OUT WITH:

Five of my classmates.

THE STRANGEST PLACE I EVER FOUND DIVINE POWER:

I was at the KTD (the Karma Triyana Dharmachakra, the Buddhist center my father helped to build), and I found this Bible and I started to read the book of Genesis (a section of the Old Testament). Even though I didn't believe in it, the writing was really powerful.

Matthew Kline

Hometown: Woodbridge, Connecticut

Age: 17

Gender: Male

School/Grade: College Freshman

Raised: Jewish

Currently: Jewish with an interest in yogic practices

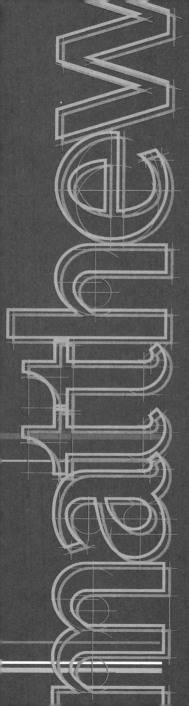

matthew

By normal teenage standards, Matthew Kline's day gets off to a pretty unusual start. He wakes at five-thirty and walks down a narrow, overgrown path to an open, squat building called the Temple. He leaves his flip-flops at the door, puts his mat on the concrete temple floor, sits down cross-legged, and meditates for thirty minutes. Then he joins others in singing some devotional songs and listens to an inspirational talk of some kind. Then, if he has time and the weather is good—and the weather in the Bahamas is always pretty good—he goes for a swim before he heads off to work.

Last January, Matt Kline was faced with a huge decision: He had fulfilled all of his high school requirements a semester early and had to figure out how to spend the rest of the school year. After a lot of thinking—and a little second-guessing—he decided to come to the Sivananda ashram in the Bahamas. (An ashram is a haven of yogic study and Hindu worship.) Matt knew that in choosing this option, he wouldn't get paid for working six days a week building new quarters, helping out in the kitchen, gardening, or doing any number of other chores at the ashram. But in exchange for his labor he would be given tasty vegetarian meals two times daily (many Hindus have a great respect for living creatures and are often vegetarian) and a bed to sleep in. He'd also be taught two important lessons that he thought he'd learned a long time ago: how to sit and how to breathe.

On the ashram, which is a kind of school for yoga (its literal translation is "place of life associated with religious exertion"), Matt is learning the physical and spiritual lessons of yoga. He's learning *pranayama*, a

what is yoga?

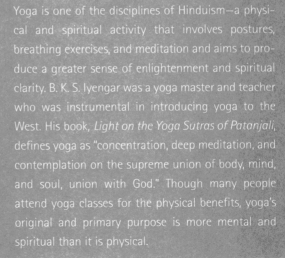

Yoga is one of the disciplines of Hinduism—a physical and spiritual activity that involves postures, breathing exercises, and meditation and aims to produce a greater sense of enlightenment and spiritual clarity. B. K. S. Iyengar was a yoga master and teacher who was instrumental in introducing yoga to the West. His book, *Light on the Yoga Sutras of Patanjali*, defines yoga as "concentration, deep meditation, and contemplation on the supreme union of body, mind, and soul, union with God." Though many people attend yoga classes for the physical benefits, yoga's original and primary purpose is more mental and spiritual than it is physical.

The instant you speak about a

series of controlled breathing exercises, and the *asanas,* ancient physical postures, which together bring purity of the body and clarity of the mind. He's also learning the mantras, the phrases that are repeated during practice and during daily life. Together these lessons have helped Matt attain the smoothness of breath and stillness of mind that allow him to sit and meditate.

The Sivananda ashram is a place where some people live and work and others go for vacation to do yoga and meditate. This is Matt's first intense spiritual practice, and his three months at the ashram have given him an interesting perspective. "They say it gives you insight," he explains. "Being here allows you to step outside your life and see yourself. Sometimes what you see is unsatisfactory. It all surfaces. At home I'm caught up in life. I don't see what I'm doing."

Though Matt still thinks of himself as a Jew—he was bar mitzvahed and regularly goes to synagogue when he's at home with his family—he's comfortable incorporating yogic practices into his Judaism. "Some of the things that yoga teaches coincide with Judaism," he says, in reference to both religions' use of prayer and meditation, their shared belief in humility before God, and their common moral ground. "So while I'm doing yoga, I'm also practicing Judaism. I'm not trying to be a better Jew by doing yoga; I'm just trying to chill out," he explains. "It's like a good side effect."

Still, Matt doesn't agree with all of the ashram's teachings. He still won't bow down to the temple altar after meditation, as is traditional, because Jewish law forbids him from bowing down to any man or any thing other than God. "I don't know that I believe everything they teach here," he admits, "but I know that what they teach is good, and a lot of it

Where desire is, there is no bliss;

matthew on practice, practice, practice:

Practicing yoga has gotten me to notice my faults, and I notice what I need to do. It's easy for me to realize what I have to work on, but it's hard to incorporate that into my life. It's like this book I'm reading, <u>Demian</u>, by Hermann Hesse. It addresses the notion that ideas aren't worth anything if you don't put them to use. So it's one thing to act compassionately and to meditate when you're on an ashram in paradise; it's another thing to apply that to the high school scene back home. The ashram isn't reality, but I hope I can keep it up and get into a routine when I get back to Connecticut.

I know to be true. I know it's a positive influence on me, and it's made me a better person."

When he goes back home after three months on the ashram, Matt says he'll undoubtedly experience a little culture shock. He'll rejoin his friends and girlfriend; there will be fast-food restaurants and televisions and automobiles. There will be proms and graduation parties, but there will also be all the bad habits he left behind. "I have a lot more self-control," he explains. "I'm not so susceptible to easy, instant gratification. I haven't made any complete resolutions, but I have more of an idea of who I want to be. I have the knowledge now. I don't know how I'll use it, but I'll sort it out. I'll play with all the different ideas and philosophies and see what works for me."

matthew

FAVORITE PLACE:

In the passenger's seat of my friend Danny's car—rolling along with my foot out the window.

FAVORITE MEAL:

Wholesome, nourishing ones.

FAVORITE JOURNEY:

My trip to the Bahamas.

GUILTY PLEASURE:

None that I feel guilty about.

MOST BOGUS MISCONCEPTION ABOUT MY BELIEFS:

That I'm pious.

FAVORITE SLOGAN, SAYING, OR SONG LYRIC:

Right now it's, "Any tool can be used as a weapon if you hold it right."

IF I FOUND A HUNDRED-DOLLAR BILL . . .

I'd do something stupid with it. I'd blow it real quick.

It is said that someone who acts as an

WHAT I MOST ADMIRE ABOUT MYSELF:

That I try and improve myself. I think about things, and I try to change them rather than surrender to them.

WHAT I LEAST ADMIRE ABOUT MYSELF:

My ego—that I like attention.

FIVE PEOPLE (LIVING OR DEAD) I'D LOVE TO HANG OUT WITH:

Bob Marley; my paternal grandfather; Swami Vishnu Sivananda, a guru; the Buddha; and my friend Bob.

enemy toward you is your best teacher.—Dalai Lama

tuesday

Tuesday (alias)
Hometown: Northern
California
Age: 16
Gender: Female
School/Grade: Junior
in High School
Raised: Vaguely Christian
Currently: Wiccan

Tuesday doesn't think of herself as a witch. She's a Wiccan, and she's heard all the <u>Sabrina</u> *and* <u>Charmed</u> *jokes before and manages to take them in stride. And while the name Tuesday is an alias used to protect her privacy, her beliefs are real. The sixteen-year-old Californian communes with nature, sleeps by the light of the moon, and even casts spells, mostly benevolent ones. She knows Wicca isn't for everyone (she's not even positive it's right for her), but the teachings and meditation and the occasional spell help her to put everything into perspective.*

religion: wicca

Founder: Unknown. In 1954 Gerald Gardner, an Englishman who said he was a witch initiated by a coven, documented the mystical traditions that make up modern-day Wicca.

History: Although this is hotly disputed by practicing Wiccans, it is assumed that Wicca is an amalgamation of several mystical traditions passed down through the ages.

Beliefs: Wiccans believe in a being or god that is too powerful for mortals to communicate with directly. Wiccans honor and worship an array of gods and goddesses who act as intermediaries between this higher power and humans, and work in union with the natural world, in conjunction with the cycles of the moon. Wicca is popular with feminists and naturalists (people who believe that elements of nature, like rocks and trees, have spirits). Some branches of Wicca are matriarchal, including only women and worshipping only goddesses. Wiccans strive to live in balance with earth and in harmony with the forces of the natural world. They value the power of the life force, communicate with creatures of the natural world, preach tolerance, and access their spiritual powers through rituals and ceremonies in nature.

Big Books: Witchcraft Today, by Gerald Gardner and *Charge of the Goddess,* by Doreen Valiente. Although Wiccans do not recognize one specific text, Book of Shadows is the name given to a book or journal of Wiccan spells that a coven or an individual creates.

House of Worship: Wiccans often meet in nature as a coven, or group of thirteen witches, to worship, work magick, and perform ceremonies.

Holidays: Most Wiccans celebrate eight different holidays: the winter and summer solstices, the vernal and autumnal equinoxes, and the four "cross-quarter days" around the first days of February, May, August, and November. Halloween is the witches' new year.

Don't doubt in the darkness what you knew

What first drew you to Wicca?

I was reading some Silver Ravenwolf, a popular Wiccan author, and she mentioned that she does magick every day. And I thought, Whoa, this is heavy-duty stuff. So in the beginning, I was in it for the magick (spells and stuff like that), the nature, and the thought of a more readily feminine religion. Also, Wicca was accepting: There is no hell if you don't obey. It's not supposed to be the one true and only way. It's loose and disorganized.

Wiccans use the old spelling magick to refer to the practical spells that they cast—for health and love and well-being—as well as more religious and mystical rituals that Wiccans employ to connect themselves to their divine power.

Were you skeptical when you first heard about it?

Yeah. I was like, "Okay, let's think about this. This could be bad. This could be like Satanism or something." I was just this kid who had no idea what she was getting into.

A lot of people don't take Wicca seriously. When did you realize it could be a legitimate spiritual pursuit?

I don't exactly remember. A lot of the Web sites had stuff to say about it, and so did the people in the Wicca news groups. They were like, "Hey! You can do what we do! It's totally legal, and we're liberal, equal rights for everyone." You can get married under Wicca and have funerals under Wicca, and it's a protected religion. I figured that if it was a protected religion, it must be legitimate.

You mentioned Wicca as a more readily feminine religion. How is it more female friendly than other religions?

In a lot of other religions the woman is subordinate to the man. Look no further than traditional Christian wedding vows: "To have and to hold; to honor and to obey." Most religions tell you that women are worth less than men, but in Wicca women and men are equal.

And there are gods and goddesses, right? Can you explain how that works?

According to Wicca, Spirit is god. It's neither male nor female but both at the same time . . . and within and without at the same time. Get what I'm saying? So Spirit is sexless but capable of taking on a lot of different forms, like male and female. There's a masculine side (the god) and a feminine side (the goddess). Each of us has a feminine and a masculine side, some more than others.

Now, the god and the goddess have different forms, and they belong to pantheons (groups of gods). There's your Greek pantheon—Zeus, Aphrodite, Pan, Athena, Prometheus, and so on. There's the Welsh pantheon: Rhiannon and friends. There's Egyptian: Isis, Osiris, Bastet, Ptah, and all those. Different witches or Wiccan practitioners work with different pantheons, and you can even interchange them if you know what you're doing.

And there's an emphasis on living in balance with the natural world, right?

Wicca is all about nature and the universe and living in harmony. Compare it to an old farm out in the middle of Any State, USA, where the cows and the pigs are all happy and well cared for, and birds come by, and it's sunny and warm and housework is done singing. It seems like home, doesn't it? Living Wicca is like honoring nature. You're supposed to respect and honor your natural surroundings while at the same time not being afraid to use them for your benefit (as long as you don't harm anything). You can grow herbs for spell uses. You can bond with animals, both wild and domestic.

All that is needed for evil to triumph

Were you raised in a religious family?

I had a loose religious upbringing. We celebrated Christmas but never went to church, ever. As a child I thought a lot about God, but once I grew older, I thought, To heck with this. I was agnostic, then I became atheistic, and now I'm Wiccan.

Is there a Wiccan slogan that you live by?

I believe in the threefold law, that whatever you do comes back to you times three. I'm not saying that if you give a dollar to charity, you'll find three on your dining-room table when you get home, but maybe you'll feel the value of giving those three dollars away, or someone will do you a nice little favor.

Some people are concerned about the magickal aspect of Wicca. Does your family give you a hard time?

Yeah, kind of. Nobody likes it. Some of my relatives are devout Christians, and I don't doubt they will be shocked and disapproving when they eventually find out. I'm going to come out to the family when I am totally, absolutely sure this is for me. Maybe it will be in a month, maybe in a year—whenever I'm ready.

So you're not absolutely sure yet?

Wicca may not be for me. I think that's true of anyone in any religion no matter how set they are in their ways. There are always religious experiences and epiphanies that can affect anyone of any religion. I might decide I like the ways of Buddhism better, or my Mormon friend might just think about switching over to Islam. Do you see what I'm saying? Everyone, everywhere, is changing all the time. Growing. If not in body, then in mind, and if not in mind, then in emotion. Opinions change. Everything changes—rocks are eroded, the earth turns; people are born, grow old, and die right in front of you. I myself decided agnosticism (I define that as not claiming to know God's ways or whether he/she/they even exist) was not for me and chose to be an atheist around the sixth grade. That didn't stop me from praying when my cousin developed cancer or thanking God when she was successfully cured. And I believe that changed me into believing something was out there again, and I found what I believe that something to be.

What do you think of the way witchcraft is portrayed in pop culture?

I don't like to see movies like *The Craft* or watch *Sabrina* on TV. They give people a false idea of what Wiccans are and what we do, and that means discrimination. If there were shows or movies like that about other religions, they'd contribute to the discrimination against those religions or they'd even be kicked off the air. If everyone knew what Wiccans do and do not do, those shows and movies would be fun to laugh at, but unfortunately, witchcraft itself has not fully emerged from the broom closet.

God, sometimes you just

WHAT ABOUT AT SCHOOL? DO PEOPLE EVER CALL YOU A POSEUR?

I may seem like a poseur—I know that some of my friends think I am. I mean, Wicca is a popular thing and really cliché among teenage girls. But you have to keep in mind that other religions can be grouped accordingly. Youth-group Christians, teen-boy agnostics, and so on.

HAVE YOUR STUDIES OF WICCA PUT YOU MORE IN TOUCH WITH NATURE?

Well, before Wicca, I didn't notice Isis and Osiris, the jays outside who were raising their family. Now I've given them names. I talk to them and often find myself outside in their presence. Now I notice how the full moon gets higher in the sky during the winter and sinks on the horizon during the summer. The night sky is of special importance to me, and once I swam in Lake Tahoe and just reveled at the sights and all. These miracles of nature have confirmed what Wicca has been teaching me: that nature is really awe inspiring and worthy of love and worship.

tuesday on her heroes:

You mean like gods and goddesses? Bastet (the Egyptian cat goddess) definitely and Isis (the Egyptian goddess of motherhood and fertility) for what she went through at the hands of Zeus and his vengeful wife. (I have the story somewhere.) I love Greek mythology, so Hecuba, the Queen of Troy who tried to protect her sons during the Trojan War, would be one, even though she was probably fictional. I like strong women and anyone who has persevered through their suffering, regardless of sex.

FAVORITE PLACE:

Okay, let's see. Either in my garden, in my room, or in my bed, all curled up with a million blankets piled on top of me and about three or four pillows.

FAVORITE MEAL:

Anything healthy and vegetarianish piques my interest so long as it tastes good. My ideal meal is a "munchies" assortment of strawberries, cherries, orange sections, pineapple slices, kiwi halves, and watermelon slices, with an entrée of something spicy. Taco casserole, mmmm. And then a salad of spinach or romaine, with ranch dressing.

FAVORITE JOURNEY:

Meditation and astral travel, without a doubt.

Astral travel is the term for allowing your soul to ascend higher than the material world.

GUILTY PLEASURE:

Uh, how guilty? Okay, let's call it "meat" and "saturated fat."

MOST BOGUS MISCONCEPTION ABOUT MY BELIEFS:

That I'm weird and I wiggle my nose like Samantha from *Bewitched* and that I'm into manipulative love spells and dramatic *90210*-ish witchy activities.

FAVORITE SLOGAN, SAYING, OR SONG LYRIC:

"Standin' on a corner in Winslow, Arizona / Such a fine sight to see / It's a girl my Lord in a flatbed Ford / Slowin' down to take a look at me" —The Eagles

IF I FOUND A HUNDRED-DOLLAR BILL . . .

I'd spend it on car insurance! Or witchcraft supplies. Or on a health club.

I'd eat pizza every day at school or drive off to McDonald's and bring lunch back.

WHAT I MOST ADMIRE ABOUT MYSELF:

Call it *la fille bohème*. My daring to be different.

WHAT I LEAST ADMIRE ABOUT MYSELF:

My self-consciousness. ("Oh God! I made a face like I was going to sneeze and then didn't, and now people around me think I'm weird!")

FIVE PEOPLE (LIVING OR DEAD) I'D LOVE TO HANG OUT WITH:

I'd love to hang out with: Stevie Nicks; my on-line friends; Don Henley; all my current friends; and my eighth-grade teacher, who died of cancer last September. Oops—that's more than five.

THE STRANGEST PLACE I EVER FOUND DIVINE POWER:

In my own backyard. I swear to Goddess. You wouldn't believe how much magick lurks on our property. Roses, clover, ivy. An anthill, a family of western scrub jays, a pair of crows who shriek all morning. Ladybug larvae that go into little cocoons and turn into ladybugs. Hummingbirds. Little autumnal pools in the front yard, near the sidewalk, that stay all winter.

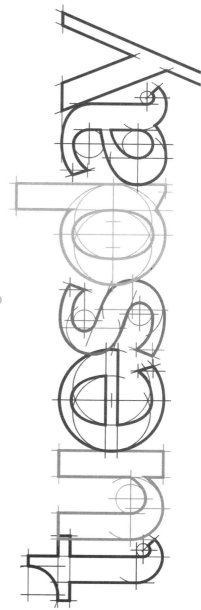

Anne Linton
Hometown: Salt Lake City, Utah
Age: 14
Gender: Female
School/Grade: Freshman in High School
Raised: The Church of Jesus Christ of Latter-Day Saints
(Mormon)
Currently: The Church of Jesus Christ of Latter-Day
Saints (Mormon)

anne

Anne Linton says she's grateful for several things: for having good parents, a close family (she has five brothers and a sister-in-law), and her membership in The Church of Jesus Christ of Latter-Day Saints. But this hasn't been the best year for Anne. Her older brother, Steve, died tragically a year ago. It was hard on everyone in Anne's family—but Anne knows she'll be with Steve again in heaven. And that might be what she's most grateful for.

religion: the church of jesus christ of latter-day saints (or mormons)

Founder: Joseph Smith

History: When Joseph Smith was 14 years old, he prayed to God to ask him which church he should join. God's response was that the church Jesus had established when he was on earth had been lost, and he asked young Smith, then living in upstate New York, to rebuild Christ's church on earth. Smith then began working toward forming the Church of Jesus Christ of Latter-Day Saints. But by the mid-nineteenth century, dogged by religious persecution, Smith and his followers were forced to flee upstate New York to Ohio and eventually to Utah to find the freedom to worship.

Beliefs: The beliefs of Latter-Day Saints (or LDS, as they call themselves) are based on the Christian model of one God who sacrificed his only son so that believers could enjoy eternal life in heaven. At baptism, Mormons commit to live a Christian life, serving their families, church, and community. Mormons believe that if married/blessed by the proper authority, families can live together even after death. Most Mormons between the ages of 19 and 21 serve an 18-month to two-year mission for the church. Paying their own way, they travel to a different state or country to teach people about their church and provide humanitarian service.

Big Books: Mormons accept the teachings of the Bible as well as the Book of Mormon. The prophets in the Book of Mormon provide insight and an additional witness into the divinity of Christ and his mission as the redeemer of the world.

House of Worship: Church for weekly worship, temple for special ceremonies like marriage.

My belief in life after death has really helped me since my brother died. I like knowing that we will be together as a family forever. I mean, he and I will get to see each other again. It's another great blessing that I have. It's not like there's nothing to hold on to; it's not like, "He's dead, okay?" When our parents were married, it was sealed in the temple and that means that the children they have are sealed to them, and so we'll all live together in heaven.

To know that Christ has died so that we may live forever, that he atoned for our sins—that's really helped me, too. It helps me to know that I can repent and be forgiven and that those sins I've repented will be blotted out. I'm grateful for the atonement of Jesus Christ, and I'm grateful for my family and the guidance of the Scriptures. We have the Book of Mormons; we have the Bible.

I also appreciate my time at the temple. I feel total elation when I'm there, like nothing else matters. When you're at the temple, you put your world on hold, and you're just ready to share the blessings you find there with others. It's a very comforting place because you know that nothing can hurt you. You feel really safe, secure, and loved.

Everyone is welcome to go to church on Sunday and worship. You have to be over 12 to go to the temple. When you're ready, you testify (profess to a bishop) your faith in Jesus and promise to follow the commandments. Each year you express your faith in Jesus and promise to keep the commandments so you can continue to go to the temple. And when you're at the temple, you feel worthy knowing that you have earned your testimony in a way. I probably feel closest to God when I'm there. I get this feeling of peace. I also feel close to Him when I pray in the morning. I say a personal prayer and a family prayer. Your personal prayer is just between you and God, while the family prayer is a blessing that you as a family need. We use the terms "thee" and "thou" and "thy" and address God as Heavenly Father, but it's not a set prayer. It's like giving thanks for food and shelter—whatever you happen to be grateful for.

prayer

Prayer is defined as offering worship, requests, confessions, or having other communications with higher powers. But the way in which it is carried out differs from person to person and religion to religion. Mormons, as well as members of many other religions, use prayer to give thanks and ask for blessings. Prayer is a deeply personal communication. It can be done publicly or privately, with words or simply with thoughts, while sitting down or standing up or kneeling on the ground. Tibetan Buddhists often use flags (which they focus on as they blow in the wind), prayer wheels (which are spun around and around so that the repetition of the movement calms their minds and helps them focus on their prayers or mantras), or mala beads (which they use to count their mantras during prayer). Roman Catholics have rosary beads, which are used to help them keep track

of the prayers called rosaries. Muslims pray five times a day—at dawn, noon, midafternoon, sundown, and nightfall—by getting on their knees and prostrating themselves in the direction of the holy city of Mecca.

Be joyful in hope, patient in affliction,

anne on house rules:

Each Mormon family has their own little rules: like I can't see PG-13 movies and some of my friends can. I can't watch certain TV shows, either. But I definitely realize that there's no benefit to watching those kinds of things. It brings me down rather than lifts me up. It takes away from that good feeling that I carry with me—we call it the Holy Ghost, and we receive it when we're baptized.

anne on sharing her faith:

One of my friends wasn't very active in my church, and I helped her to get back into it and she's really grateful now. Sometimes I think about what the Gospel would do for others and I want to share it with them, but I don't want to be like, "Oh, you have to join." I think that's wrong.

I like that Mormons have really strong values. We don't swear, and I think that's a really positive thing—it just makes it nicer to be around people. I've also noticed that LDS people have a spark in their eyes. People who are very spiritual in our church, like our prophet, they just have a twinkle in their eye, and it's sort of special. Some people tell me I have that spark. I hope so.

FAVORITE PLACE:

Nature.

FAVORITE MEAL:

Breakfast.

FAVORITE JOURNEY:

Being at the LDS Young Women's Camp.

GUILTY PLEASURE:

I love strawberry daiquiris—nonalcoholic!

MOST BOGUS MISCONCEPTION PEOPLE HAVE ABOUT MY BELIEFS:

That Mormons are perfect and we think we're better than others.

FAVORITE SLOGAN, SAYING, OR SONG LYRIC:

"The most universal quality is diversity."

IF I FOUND A HUNDRED-DOLLAR BILL . . .

I would pay my tithing (a regular contribution to the church) first, decide how much to spend and how much to save, then go shopping for a cushion for my chair, things for friends like picture frames or lip gloss or nail polish, and a swimsuit for me.

WHAT I MOST ADMIRE ABOUT MYSELF:

That I'm an open, friendly person with high standards.

WHAT I LEAST ADMIRE ABOUT MYSELF:

I can be impatient and take offense about things.

FIVE PEOPLE (LIVING OR DEAD) I'D LOVE TO HANG OUT WITH:

Joseph, of the Bible; Ammon, from the Book of Mormons; my brother Steve; Enoch, from the Bible; and Jesus Christ.

Nathan Harrington
Hometown: Rockville, Maryland
Age: 16
Gender: Male
School/Grade: Junior in
           High School
Raised: Quaker
Currently: Quaker

As long as he can remember, Nathan Harrington has been a Quaker. Just about every Sunday since he was a little kid, he and his family have attended the Quaker meetinghouse in Sandy Spring, Maryland, to sit and meditate. Nathan likes being a Quaker; he's proud of the emphasis on political activism, the long-standing commitment to nonviolence, and the acceptance and recognition of all other religions. What he really likes is that once he settles in on the hard wooden benches of the meetinghouse, no one tells him what to do or what to think. He simply closes his eyes and finds the spirit on his own.

religion: quaker
(or society of friends)

Founder: George Fox

History: The Quaker religion began in England in 1650 when George Fox rejected conventional Christianity, with its ornate churches and clergymen, and founded the Society of Friends on the presumption that clergy were unnecessary middlemen between the faithful and God. Quakerism was established in colonial America by William Penn, who also founded the state of Pennsylvania.

Beliefs: Quakers believe that each individual should cultivate his/her own relationship with God through meditation. Most Friends, as they are sometimes called, adhere to strict nonviolence, believing that since there is God in everyone, life is sacred. Before the Civil War, Quakers were instrumental in the Underground Railroad movement, through which many southern slaves escaped to the North. Quaker meetinghouses are modest and unadorned, and Quakers' weekly meetings include no formal ceremony, no clergy, and no music so as not to distract from direct communication with God. Followers are called Quakers because they were once said "to tremble or quake at the word of God." Originally, Quakers avoided luxury and emphasized simplicity in dress, manners, and speech. Quakers have always been committed to non-violence and political activism. They were outspoken abolitionists and have consistently objected to every war the United States has ever been involved with. They believe in a universal brother/sisterhood, equality regardless of sex, race, or age, and an unwavering commitment to truth and simplicity.

House of Worship: Meetinghouse.

Seek justice, encourage the oppressed. Defend the cause

What, aside from its commitment to nonviolence and its political activism, makes Quakerism appealing to you?

Well, the fact that each person follows their own spiritual path and that anyone can achieve revelation and inspiration on their own. In our services we speak to each other rather than being spoken to by a single minister. Also, Quakers believe that all religions are legitimate. There's the recognition that there are many paths to heaven, God, enlightenment, nirvana, whatever you will.

You were raised Quaker. Have the principles you've been taught stayed with you?

I do try to be mindful of my conduct and the principles of Quakerism, but I don't always succeed. I think Quakers in general are fairly focused on their conduct and are conscious of applying Quaker principles to their lives. But it's strange because we're not really *told* how to conduct ourselves.

What do you mean?

I'm not told how to conduct myself, but I'm constantly listening to what other people say, the revelations they have had, and watching how they conduct themselves.

You mentioned that there is no minister at Meetings and that people just speak to each other. What if no one speaks?

The idea is to sit and reflect, worship, and meditate: settle the mind and still the soul. Sometimes I have things on my mind and I just need to relax, so I just close my eyes and think pleasant thoughts. Other times I can get kind of restless. But the best times in meeting are when there's something that I'm trying to work through. I sort of meditate or pray or just send good vibes and hope that the best will come out of it. It's like seeking guidance, you know? Anyway, you sit and reflect, and if you feel inspired to speak, you stand up and share what you have to say. The idea is that you should speak not when you personally have something to say but when you feel that the spirit (or the Inner Light, as Quakers often refer to God) is speaking through you.

How do you know when the spirit is speaking through someone?

For the most part, whatever people say is accepted. To claim that what they said was not an appropriate message is to presume that their words were not truly spiritually inspired—and that's a big presumption to make.

Have you ever spoken in a meeting?

I've only spoken once. It was a big experience for me. There was a tragic death in the community—a friend of mine, Matthew, died at age 17 in a sort of freak accident. The whole school went to his funeral, which was at a Catholic church. It was a pretty nice service, but because most of the people there weren't Catholic, they didn't particularly relate to what the priest was saying. He said something about how Matthew's life allowed us to know Jesus Christ. And I thought, I wonder what he means by that because Matthew wasn't that religious a guy; he didn't go around telling people about Jesus. Then I realized that a lot of the people there were probably wondering the same thing. After I thought about it, it occurred to me that the priest was just talking about the things that Jesus supposedly embodied, the love and the compassion and so forth. Those are things that Matthew certainly did exhibit, and by doing that he helped make us understand the importance of those qualities.

You brought this up in Meeting?

I got up and explained what I just explained to you. I then went on to say that a lot of times, when people are talking about religion, they get hung up on terminology and diction when they don't need to. I knew that some people would describe what the priest said as Bible-thumping nonsense, but I explained that if they looked beyond the terminology to the meaning,

Prayer is the key to Heaven,

they would find that they totally agreed with his message, and they'd see a glimpse of the enormous commonality between different religions. That's the content of what I said, but the amazing thing is that when I said it in that meeting worship, I said it much better than I could ever express it before or since. Somehow it just had a clarity about it.

ARE QUAKERS ENCOURAGED TO EXPLORE OTHER RELIGIONS?

Yeah, definitely. In the third and fourth grades they have us read the Bible, and then in fifth and sixth grades we study comparative religion or religion in general. You know, a lot of Quakers consider themselves Christians; some are agnostics; some have Buddhist leanings. (Originally the Quaker church was founded on a belief in Jesus Christ. But since the religion is noncreedal, Friends hold a large spectrum of belief.)

COULD YOU EVER SEE YOURSELF PURSUING ANOTHER RELIGION?

I don't think I can make that prediction. I know I'll never abandon Quakerism completely, but I might incorporate some other religion into Quakerism.

nathan on activism:

There's a long tradition of Quakers being politically active; there's always someone at our meetinghouse who is organizing a protest or some kind of political action. It's inspired me to get involved in causes like campaigns against militarization and economic injustice and to push for things like universal health care and an end to the United States' bombing of other countries for so-called humanitarian intervention.

FAVORITE PLACE:

Piazza del Duomo, Florence, Italy.

FAVORITE MEAL:

Maryland crab cakes with french fries.

FAVORITE JOURNEY:

From crazy rebel to brave intellectual.

GUILTY PLEASURE:

Playing air guitar.

MOST BOGUS MISCONCEPTION ABOUT MY BELIEFS:

People think Quakers are the same as the Amish or the Shakers.

The Shakers believe that a woman named Ann Lee was a female representation of Jesus Christ. Their worship often involves such intense bodily experience that they shake, and they value celibacy over marriage. The Amish, who are Protestant, maintain an agricultural way of life, dressing in plain clothes and not using electricity or other modern inventions.

FAVORITE SLOGAN, SAYING, OR SONG LYRIC:

"O body swayed to music, O brightening glance, How can we know the dancer from the dance?" —W. B. Yeats, *Among School Children*.

He who pursues righteousness and love

IF I FOUND A HUNDRED-DOLLAR BILL . . .

I'd donate it to the War Resisters League.

WHAT I'D REALLY DO:

Buy cheesy poofs and candy corn.

WHAT I MOST ADMIRE ABOUT MYSELF:

My political consciousness and activism.

WHAT I LEAST ADMIRE ABOUT MYSELF:

My impulsiveness.

FIVE PEOPLE (LIVING OR DEAD) I'D LOVE TO HANG OUT WITH:

Jesus; labor organizer and activist Eugene Debs; Albert Einstein; Andy Kaufman; and Michael Stipe.

THE STRANGEST PLACE I EVER FOUND DIVINE POWER:

In the principal's office after a suspension.

finds life, prosperity, and honor. —Proverbs 21:21

Mary Angela Moutoussis

Hometown: New York, New York

Age: 15

Gender: Female

School/Grade: Sophmore at The Brearley
School

Raised: Greek Orthodox

Currently: Greek Orthodox

mary angela

Mary Angela is a girl with a lot on her plate. She plays tennis and soccer, and she's got tons of extracurriculars and, of course, loads of schoolwork. The pressure is always there—to do well in school, excel at sports, get involved at church, and find time with her friends. But Mary Angela does have a place to go to get away—a no-pressure zone with soothing music, good people, and a really great vibe.

religion:
greek orthodox

History: Like Roman Catholicism, the Greek Orthodox Church was founded at Pentecost in 33 A.D., after the death and resurrection of Jesus Christ. In 1054 A.D., the Western (Latin) and Eastern (Greek) branches separated (the period is called the Great Schism) and followed separate courses. The Western Church of Rome (which is now the Roman Catholic Church) continues to be ruled by the Pope, while the Church of Constantinople and the other Eastern Orthodox Churches reject papal primacy infallibility and are a communion of self-governing churches. The Eastern Orthodox Church includes the Greek, Russian, Middle Eastern, Central, and Eastern European Churches.

Beliefs: The Greek Orthodox Church believes in the classical Christian teachings of the resurrection of Jesus Christ, the Trinity (the doctrine of God as three persons: the Father, the Son, and the Holy Spirit), the Bible, ritual worship, and the holy icons.

Big Books: The Bible, the Nicene Creed (a type of vow), and the seven Ecumenical Councils (Christian assemblies).

Holidays: Greek Orthodox churches celebrate the Sabbath, the major Christian holidays such as Easter and Christmas, and most other holy days. They generally follow a different calendar from other Western Christians.

I pray every night, but I definitely feel closest to God when I'm in our church. It's the atmosphere. There's something about just being in church with the people and the liturgy and the music that relaxes you. It's usually calm, and there's peaceful music that just kind of soothes your soul. It's not like pop or rock—you can't really listen to rock and pray you know what I mean? The peaceful music distracts your mind from your surroundings so you can concentrate on talking to God.

Give thanks and praise to the Lord

People in the Greek Orthodox community aren't always very close, but when we're all praying together in church, you get a different sense. The church is kind of like a haven where everyone can just come and pray and get everything out. They don't feel like they're being judged or like they have to hide their personalities. I've also been praying every night before I go to bed for as long as I can remember—usually the Lord's Prayer. And then I'll add certain things at the end, relating to what's happening in my life or what's happened during the day. I can talk to God about things I can't normally talk to my parents or my friends about. I guess that's one of the benefits of praying. I usually ask Him to help me make the right decisions when I have to, and it pretty much goes from there—although I guess I rely on my inner self to make the right decision when the time comes. I play soccer and tennis, and I'm a triathlete, so I run and swim and bike. I do lots of extracurricular activities: I play the piano; I teach at school; I'm involved in the church. So sometimes I just pray that I can go through the next week calmly and take it step by step. I ask Him to help me so that I don't get too stressed.

My relationship with God is completely isolated from what I've read in the Bible and what I've learned in Sunday school, where I've been going since I was five. When I ask God to help me make those everyday decisions, I can't find any text in the Bible that relates to that. But I think that as I get older, the Bible and the Scriptures are going to start playing a bigger role in my spirituality.

Easter is the most important holiday for the Greek Orthodox community. I'll usually give up something for Lent (the forty days of atonement preceding Easter), but what I give up varies from year to year. On Clean Monday—that's the first Monday in Lent—we give up meat, and then a couple of weeks before Easter we give up cheese. The last week before Easter we're supposed to barely eat anything, just liquids and soup and beans. By not eating meat and cheese, we isolate ourselves even more from all the materialistic things that we have around us, but for me it doesn't really work this way.

My spiritual relationship is there no matter what—and giving up these things doesn't add to it at all. Still, it's an offering, an opportunity to show my devotion to God because that's how I've been brought up. This is how I'm supposed to show my devotion. And if I can show it to Him, I will.

My school, where I learn to work with my friends to overcome challenges.

FAVORITE MEAL:

Lobster from Maine. I also enjoy fried eggplant and zucchini with tzatziki (a Greek tradition).

FAVORITE JOURNEY:

Smelling the fresh brisk air and pine trees on our way to Vermont in the winter to ski, where the shimmering snow traps the noise.

GUILTY PLEASURE:

I like staying in bed late listening to the radio.

FAVORITE SLOGAN, SAYING, OR SONG LYRIC:

"Every exit is an entry somewhere else."—Tom Stoppard

IF I FOUND A HUNDRED-DOLLAR BILL . . .

I would use it for shopping.

mary angela on destiny:

I believe that God has planned every decision and every act that we are going to take part in before we're even born. He knows everything that's going to happen. Since I can't tell my future, I kind of rely on Him and ask Him to lead me through my decisions. I believe that my destiny is in God's hands. It's a comfort, even though I don't know what that destiny is.

I do not pray for success,

mary angela

WHAT I MOST ADMIRE ABOUT MYSELF:

My willpower and my morals.

WHAT I LEAST ADMIRE ABOUT MYSELF:

I wish I were a better student and an MVP athlete

FIVE PEOPLE (LIVING OR DEAD) I'D LOVE TO HANG OUT WITH:

My two grandfathers; Jesus; Mia Hamm; and Prince William.

THE STRANGEST PLACE I'VE EVER FOUND DIVINE POWER:

Walking up the stairs on the way to a math test.

I ask for faithfulness. —Mother Teresa

Jess McIntosh
Hometown: Washington, D.C.
Age: 18
Gender: Male
School/Grade: High School Senior
Raised: Methodist
Currently: Unaffiliated

jess

Somewhere in the middle of his junior year of high school, Jess McIntosh hit rock bottom. When he stepped back and took a look at the things he was doing and his life at school, it all felt superficial and shallow. Jess got distant and angry. Already drinking heavily, Jess began to experiment with drugs. He quickly formed a chemical dependency and fell into a deep depression. But now, a year later, things are looking up—and Jess says he has God to thank. . . .

Junior year was really tough for me. Somewhere in the middle of that year some sort of switch flipped. I took a step back from everything and started observing what actually went on with my friends and my life at school. And it all just seemed so trivial and trite—it just threw me for a loop. It seemed like people didn't care about anything more than a good party on the weekend and kissing up to some teacher to get an A. My school is extremely sheltered—it felt like people were oblivious to everything else that goes on in the world. And I was the same way. I felt really useless just going to school and not really doing much and not contributing to anything. So I started feeling disgruntled with everything and unhappy with my situation. I became depressed and mopey and grumpy. I withdrew from my family; I drank more than I should have and experimented with drugs—it was a bad stage of my life. Everything was just overwhelming. I wasn't able to separate other people's problems from my own, and so I kind of took the whole world on my shoulders. It was just too much to handle, and it sent me into this tailspin in terms of substance abuse. By senior year I was an addict. One night I took ecstasy and mushrooms and I got completely separated from reality. I ended up having to go to the hospital. I guess I kind of had a near-death experience. It was really frightening.

Afterward I kept getting these awful panic attacks, and one night I could actually feel myself sort of dying. Every bone in my body was convinced that I was about to die. I was extremely frightened and I started to pray, and there was something about it that was different than all the kinds of prayers I'd said before. This time every ounce of concentration and energy in my body was devoted to speaking with God. Then—I can't really explain it—this wave of comfort came over me and gave me the sense that I wasn't completely alone.

For a long time I had felt completely separated from everyone else in this world. But that night God gave me this sense of not being alone, and from that point on I've taken my spirituality very seriously. I'm convinced that I've been saved, that God had mercy on me. I had a dream where an angel—I know this all sounds really stupid—an angel spoke to me and said, "We're gonna give you a second chance, but it's going to be the hardest fight of your life." And it really has been.

I've learned an incredible amount from the experience. I was teetering on the edge of oblivion, but my spirituality really helped me get through the awful times that I'd brought upon myself. I was raised Methodist, so I've always had a spiritual base that I've sort of relied on. But for a while there, I lost it. I'd always prayed every night, but it got to be kind of mechanical—a just-in-case sort of thing. It's

Heavy thoughts bring on physical maladies;

amazing how much my life has changed since then. I don't pray more often now, but when I do pray, I try to mean it.

I always kind of figured that everyone's spirituality is a very personal, individual type of thing, so I've never really been into organized religion like my parents. I think there's a lot more to be gained from personal reflection and developing your own philosophies about the world around you. Which is what I try to do—I've started trying to open myself up to other people. I've started trying to just focus on the beautiful parts of everybody. For some reason, it's really easy for me to dwell on the negatives, so I have to work to put those aside. I've started listening to the music between the notes, the endless possibilities. That's kind of what God is, I guess. I make an effort to appreciate every moment I've been given and to do the best I can so that later on, I can say that I deserved my second chance and that I actually did something with it.

jess on christianity:

I don't really see myself as exclusively Christian. I've taken a couple of courses in Eastern religions, and if I see something I like in another religion, I guess I kind of cut and paste it into my own. I'm working on forming my own spirituality. The most spiritual thing, for me, is getting out in the world and into nature, going on a walk through the woods by my house. That's the kind of thing that sets me straight most of the time.

jess on the future:

I'm going to defer college for a year. In the fall I'm going to Africa and the Middle East with a program called Youth International to work with AIDS relief organizations and Habitat for Humanity.

FAVORITE PLACE:

A hill near my home that looks out over Washington, D.C. Unfortunately, it's being bulldozed and built on, so it will soon be no longer.

FAVORITE MEAL:

Give me squash, brussels sprouts, spinach, pinto beans with rice, and soy meat, and I'll be a happy man. I'm a vegetarian, and I try to adhere to a macrobiotic diet—it's not the most exciting food, but I love it.

FAVORITE JOURNEY:

Driving around the country by myself. I just love to see the world around me on my own time and schedule. I get lonely at times, but the trips prove to be great therapy.

GUILTY PLEASURE:

I used to have much worse guilty pleasures, but now I would say my favorite is lying in bed all day just listening to the radio, reading, or sleeping.

Trust in Him at all times; ye people, pour out your

MOST BOGUS MISCONCEPTION ABOUT MY BELIEFS:

That they promote selfishness. I find beauty in the range of human emotions and experiences, and I believe it's everyone's duty to immerse themselves in all facets of humanity, from self-restriction to self-indulgence.

FAVORITE SAYING, SLOGAN, OR SONG LYRIC:

"When life gets hard and you've lost your dreams, there's nothing like a campfire and a can of beans."—Tom Waits

IF I FOUND A HUNDRED-DOLLAR BILL . . .

I would spend it on new music.

WHAT I MOST ADMIRE ABOUT MYSELF:

My thoughtfulness.

WHAT I LEAST ADMIRE ABOUT MYSELF:

My impatience.

FIVE PEOPLE (LIVING OR DEAD) I'D LOVE TO HANG OUT WITH:

Albert Camus; Beck; Tom Waits; Will Ferrell, from *Saturday Night Live*; and Leonard Cohen.

STRANGEST PLACE I EVER FOUND DIVINE POWER:

In the waiting room at my doctor's office. I don't know why; I just got that feeling.

conclusion

So what is spirituality?

Is it belief in a god? An awareness of the possibilities of the universe? A commitment to stand by religious traditions?

For Britt, it's a personal relationship with Jesus. For Lunar Dragon, it's a connection to the mystical. For Tuesday, it's finding harmony and balance with the natural world. For each one of these teens and—in fact—for everyone, everywhere, it means something different.

This book has only scratched the surface of those meanings. And it has provided only a tiny glimpse into some of the different faiths that exist all over the world. But, hopefully, these interviews and essays have made one thing clear: that no matter how we're raised and what we're taught, only we get to choose what we truly believe.